# Canoeing and Kayaking

## for Persons with Physical Disabilities

## Instruction Manual

by Anne Wortham Webre and Janet Zeller

Published by the
American Canoe Association, Inc.
8580 Cinderbed Road, Suite 1900
P.O. Box 1190
Newington, VA 22122-1190
703/550-7495

Library of Congress Catalog Card Number: 90-83762
ISBN 0-943117-02-X

The American Canoe Association (ACA), founded in
1880, continues today as the oldest national canoeing
organization in the world and as one of the oldest
national sports governing bodies in North America.

The ACA is dedicated to water safety and to the
promotion of the various forms of canoeing as sport
and recreation. Through its National Activity
Committees, the ACA promotes recreation,
conservation, instruction, and sanctions and governs
flatwater and whitewater canoe and kayak racing in
the United States. The Disabled Paddlers Committee of
the ACA promotes the participation of paddlers with
physical disabilities in all areas of canoeing, kayaking,
and coastal kayaking. The proceeds from this manual
will help continue the work of the Disabled Paddlers
Committee.

Printed in the United States of America

# In Appreciation

The Charles Butcher Foundation for its support and sponsorship.

The many paddlers and instructors who have shared their expertise and suggestions with us.

Our families and friends for their unending support and encouragement.

For permission to use their information:
Michael Arthur and Stacy Ackroyd-Stolarz, authors of the Canadian Recreation Canoeing Association's  A Resource Manual On Canoeing For Disabled People.

Geoff Smedley, author of the British Canoe Union's  A Guide To Canoeing With Disabled Persons.

**Advisors:**
Judy Hammond and Gordon Grant
 of the Nantahala Outdoor Center.
Syd Jacobs and John Galland,
 both experienced paddlers with disabilities.

**Specialization Editors:**
Grace and Jack Beigle: Open Canoeing
Chris Bullard: Physical Therapy
Dinsmore DeVoto and Elizabeth Scott-Graham:
 Grammar
Dr. Howard Drucker: Special Education
Rene´ Ennulat: Recreational Therapy
Dr. Kathleen Long: Medical Information
Anita Marchitelli and Sarah Geer: Hearing
 Impairment
Pat McGowen: Pharmacy
Patty Norvelle: Flatwater Kayaking
Stephen Parsons: Risk Management
Dr. Charles Sutherland: Coastal Kayaking
Laura Kate Webre: Whitewater Kayaking

# TABLE OF CONTENTS

## CREDITS

**Editor:**
Laurie Gullion
**Illustrator:**
Louis Casey
**Graphic Design:**
Spencer & Benson Graphic Arts
**Photography:**
Holly Zeller, Neil Webre
Cover photograph
of able/disabled sea
kayaking trip off
Odiorne Point,
New Hampshire

Hello!

A little background is needed before you get into the manual.

This manual is full of information that needs to be shared. It provides unique information dealing with physical disabilities and paddling, which is not covered in general instruction manuals. Much of the information has been gathered from the experiences of many instructors, paddlers, and health care professionals. The goal is to increase instructional and general paddling opportunities for people with physical disabilities.

This manual is not a complete, detailed guide to all aspects of canoeing and kayaking. It is intended to supplement the technical information found in the ACA <u>Canoeing and Kayaking Instruction Manual</u> which deals with flatwater, moving water, and whitewater and also the ACA <u>Fundamentals Of Coastal Kayaking Manual For Instructors</u> which deals with open water paddling. Both are available through the ACA National Office. (Appendix 6)

We have written this manual for instructors. We know that it will also be used by many other people – paddlers with disabilities, therapists, outdoor recreation specialists, etc. That's great! We hope the information will be helpful and will encourage folks to see the possibilities in paddling. However, **reading this manual does not replace the need for good instruction. A certified instructor is your assurance of competency, your way of knowing that you are getting qualified, safe instruction.** Ask if the instructor is certified and by whom. For information about certified instructors and those who have had additional training working with paddlers with physical disabilities, contact the ACA National Office.

The authors choose the gender in which a book will be written. For ease in reading, in order to avoid the awkwardness of using she/he, his/hers and to keep everyone alert, we have chosen the feminine form. When you see "she" or "her" throughout the manual, we are referring to people, and not necessarily to women.

We feel strongly about the importance of the integration of paddlers who are able and disabled in all areas of paddling. Often an able/disabled instructional class is ideal. With the appropriate equipment adaptations in place, settled before the first class, the instruction is basically the same for all students. Through the common interest in paddling, students able and disabled get to know each other as individuals and move beyond the barriers of uncertainty and misunderstanding often created by a physical disability.

Follow the manual; it will lead the way. We have used the manual with instructors and students. The comment we keep hearing from instructors is, "Once you get the adaptations settled, the instruction is just about the same." There is more to it than that, so don't just skip to the adaptations section. Read the whole manual! These successful instructors have incorporated the guidelines, used the information and it worked.

This manual is a beginning. As more instructors and paddlers with physical disabilities work together, more refinements will develop. Great! We want to hear from you so that the next edition will be bigger and better. We welcome additional adaptations and techniques which have proven successful. The ACA Disabled Paddlers Committee Clearinghouse is set up to distribute information on helpful techniques and adaptations. The Clearinghouse is always open to new ideas — what has worked for one paddler may be just the thing another paddler needs. So please send those adaptation ideas to the American Canoe Association, Disabled Paddlers Committee. (Appendix 6)

## THE AUTHORS

### Janet Zeller:
I bring the viewpoint and experience of a paddler who is disabled. After twenty five years of paddling, mostly whitewater open canoe and wilderness trips and a few years of sea kayaking, I became disabled. I was not about to give up my paddling, so adaptation was the way to go. It has been five years and thanks to adaptations, I am still paddling my sea kayak.

The freedom I discover each time I paddle is a gift to my spirit. My husband and I often kayak off the short coastline of New Hampshire. We meet other folks on the water and often again at the take-out. They are amazed when my husband lifts me from the kayak and places me in my wheelchair. On the water I am just another sea kayaker. My equality with other paddlers is based on my skill and that feels great. As my disability increases, I change my adaptations and paddling remains my sport and my freedom.

I have worked with other paddlers with physical disabilities across the country and have seen them make the same discovery As the Chairman of the ACA Disabled Paddlers Committee, my goal for this manual is to gather and share information so that other folks with physical disabilities will also be able to experience the freedom, equality, and fun of paddling.

Special thanks to my husband, Bill; he is the wind beneath my wings, the best of partners, paddlers and instructors.

### Anne Wortham Webre:
I began paddling canoes and kayaks at Camp Merrie-Woode in Sapphire, North Carolina, thirty years ago. Most of my paddling has been on whitewater rivers. I have been an American Red Cross Canoeing instructor since 1982 and have taught water-based activities at Cal Poly, San Luis Obispo, CA for five years.

While attending a conference on outdoor leadership, I had the pleasure of attending a presentation by Tom Whittaker, founder of the Cooperative Wilderness Handicapped Outdoor Group, (C.W. HOG). I realized in listening to his talk and seeing his slides how easily paddling could be adapted to include a variety of abilities. Having been an instructor of canoeing and kayaking for many years, I decided to try to teach people with disabilities the sport that has been so much a part of my life. I approached the Wheelchair Basketball Team in San Luis Obispo, California with an offer to teach them paddling – telling them, of course, that they would be learning the paddling skills while I was learning how to adapt the equipment and instruction to best suit their abilities. Several of my friends helped with the classes and we learned by doing, often the hard way.

From 1985 to the present I have been teaching kayaking and canoeing in California on the Central Coast near Morro Bay to many people who have different disabilities. People with disabilities have been excluded from many recreational activities. We hope that this manual will make more opportunities available to them. As a spin off from using this manual, instructors and organizations providing recreational opportunities can advocate for wheelchair-accessible outdoor recreation areas, e.g. docks, camping areas, and for integrated able/disabled classes.

My special thanks to my friend and husband, Neil, for making me laugh, and to my kids for making me take twice as long to write this book.

We welcome suggestions and ideas for adaptations from readers.

*Good Paddling!*
*Annie & Janet*

September, 1990

**Annie says: Send all criticisms to Janet and all praise to Annie!**

# CHAPTER ONE

# Introduction

## WHY CANOEING AND KAYAKING?

Gliding freely across the surface of the water, experiencing wildlife, mastering new skills, exercising, choosing your own limits and recreating with friends are some of the best reasons for canoeing and kayaking. Enjoyment can be experienced from the first paddle stroke and fulfillment is found at all skill levels.

Whether it is a quiet paddle on a calm lake, the challenge of a whitewater river, touring by sea kayak, or competition, the paddler decides which type of paddling to pursue. New challenges are always available. A person needs to be willing to accept instruction, to challenge herself, and to adjust to new situations.

Paddling is a sport which emphasizes ability. Skill is determined by ability and attitude, whether the paddler is able-bodied or disabled. We are three paragraphs into this manual and now the word disabled is used for the first time. The freedom paddling offers pushes aside the barriers presented by disabilities. A body which may be uncooperative on land becomes part of a sleek craft gliding through the water. Together paddlers, able-bodied and disabled, can share all aspects of the sport. Water is the ultimate equalizer.

## A SPECIAL MANUAL

This manual is designed for the instruction of persons with physical disabilities. It contains unique information needed by instructors, paddlers, therapists, and recreation specialists. This manual offers the appropriate information and adaptations to manage the impact of a paddler's physical disability and to place the focus on the paddler's abilities.

The emphasis in instruction should always be on the ability of the paddler, within the limits of the individual's disability. That goal is not as difficult as it sounds if you use the right tools. This manual is a toolbox. It contains information and suggestions to help the instructor and paddler work together effectively.

First, the basic tools are necessary. They are used to create the framework for effective instruction: guidelines for instructors, students' abilities and instructors' attitudes, safety and risk, swimming, paddler's interview, and possible implications for paddling of the disability involved. Then use the finishing tools: adaptations, additional techniques for rescues and rolls, equipment suggestions and other tools as needed. The appendix is the extra drawer in the toolbox. It contains additional information and resources. Read and use the entire manual because each chapter offers a piece of the structure. This manual is to be used with an appropriate general canoeing/kayaking instruction manual, such as the American Canoe Association's (ACA) Canoeing and Kayaking Instruction Manual and/or the ACA's Fundamentals for Coastal Kayaking

Manual for Instructors. In combination with this manual, you can follow the recommended ACA instructional format.

### WHO IS DISABLED?

The U.S. Census Bureau reports that nearly twenty-five percent of Americans have a physical disability. A disability is a physical condition which causes a physical limitation. There are no firm statistics on the number of people with disabilities who are involved in sports. Athletes who use a wheelchair, crutches, canes, etc. are noticed, but there are many physical disabilities which are not visible. This manual includes information on a full range of disabilities. Although the body may be limited in function, a person's positive attitude can help her discover her abilities. With the emphasis on ability, the disability can be managed and the sports of canoeing and kayaking can be opened for everyone.

Provides the same interest and benefits for people with disabilities as for able-bodied
Can participate with family and friends
Emphasizes ability
Experiencing success
Provides good exercise
Challenging
Therapeutic for both mind and body
Independence
Provides a personal experience
Seeing wildlife
Developing self-confidence
Improving self-esteem
Barrier-free mobility
Fun
Learning to adjust to new situations
Experiencing group work
Enjoyable at all levels of ability
Readily available in many places
Safe and economical
Adaptations are minimal
Easily transported
Access to a variety of places
Variety of ages and abilities can enjoy it
Combines with camping, birding, fishing, etc.
Increases upper body strength and range of motion
Provides cross training for other sports.

## BENEFITS OF PADDLING

# CHAPTER TWO

# General Guidelines for Instructors

When you work with a student with a physical disability, the most important aspect of the instructor/student relationship is a positive attitude. It develops from the instructor's belief that the student can succeed and from the student's confidence in the instructor.

Sounds like any instructor/student relationship, doesn't it?

That is why the best instructors for students with disabilities are instructors who are good at teaching any student. The actual paddling skills that are taught to a student with a disability are the same as those taught to a student who is able-bodied. There are more similarities than there are differences in the instruction.

Yes, there are differences in working with a student who has a disability. The goal of the manual is to help manage the differences so the instructor will be able to concentrate on the similarities in the instruction.

## WHAT TO SAY

A couple of definitions may help. Disabled and handicapped are the two terms most commonly used to describe a person with a physical limitation. A **disability** is a medically-definable physical condition which causes a physical limitation. A **handicap** is a barrier. It may be environmental such as stairs which handicap a person in a wheelchair. Or the handicap may be a negative attitude by the individual who is disabled or by another person. So, disabled is the correct term to use when referring to a student's medically-definable physical limitation. Able-bodied is the term used to refer to an individual without such limitations.

Physically challenged, differently able, etc., are awkward terms which are often used by able-bodied folks but are not generally acceptable to people with disabilities. Those individuals who have disabilities and prefer to use another term will make their preference clear.

Whenever possible when speaking, put the person first and then the disability. For example, say the person who is hearing impaired, instead of the hearing-impaired person. The person is more important than her disability.

Do not play the "we are just alike" game. A physical disability, which is obvious, need not be ignored but it is, also, not the center of attention. The individual knows that she is disabled and the instructor knows she is disabled. Look beyond the disability and discover the individual.

**Ability** should be emphasized. What a student can do is more important than what she cannot do.

## WHAT TO DO

Discomfort often comes from not knowing what to say or how to act when confronted with a person with a disability. We have included some suggestions to keep in mind in your interactions with people with disabilities.

It is a generality, but most likely an individual who is disabled and is interested in canoeing or kayaking has probably come to grips with the limitations caused by her disability and is relatively independent. Give her room to use her ability. State once that you are willing to give any help; she need only ask. Then leave it at that. What may appear to you to be an awkward struggle, may be the individual's normal way to function. Do not keep asking "May I help you?". Once you have made a clear offer to assist, the individual will ask if she needs or wants your help. Repeated offers only indicate your discomfort with her efforts to be independent.

Now we have the terminology and good manners settled. Let's continue!

## SAFETY AND RISK

Safety is always a concern. The issue of safety is the same for all students whether they are able-bodied or disabled. That is, a competent instructor makes the safety of all students a top priority at all times and introduces new skills, risks, and challenges only as each student is ready for them.

Risk is a concern for everyone, but the element of risk is often exaggerated by disability. For some people with disabilities, risk is the adventurous edge to the sport that gives a sense of satisfaction and raises the individual's self-esteem. Risk for all paddlers must be managed at an acceptable level. It is the instructor's responsibility to inform the paddler of the risks involved. The paddler who is disabled has a right to risk so long as she is aware of the risks. The ultimate decision

## Tips for Interacting with People with Disabilities.

- Remember that people are still people, despite disabilities.
- Relax.
- Look directly at the person; maintain eye contact.
- When having a long conversation with a person who is in a wheelchair, stoop down or sit nearby so that you are closer to the same eye level.
- Do not lean on or use a person's wheelchair, crutches, etc. without permission.
- Ask first if assistance is needed; do not assume.
- Speak as you would normally. If you are speaking to a person who has a mobility impairment, you do not need to avoid words like run, walk, etc.
- When speaking to a person who is hearing impaired, be sure she has a clear view of your mouth. Keep hands, food, etc. away from your mouth while you are speaking. Ideally, mustaches should be cut short in order for the upper lip to be seen. Shouting makes lip reading more difficult.
- When speaking to a person who is visually-impaired, be sure to introduce yourself. Use the clock method to assist the person in locating or avoiding something. The clock method uses the numbers on the clock for reference points: straight in front of the person is 12:00; directly in back is 6:00.
- Don't shout! Most people with disabilities have normal hearing.

to participate belongs to the individual whether disabled or able.

The perception of risk varies. The individual who has never paddled may perceive a flatwater lake as high risk. However, with previous paddling experience, whitewater paddling may appear easily manageable. Open, comfortable communication between the student and instructor is vital to discerning the student's perception of risk and thereby being prepared for her reaction. Good communication is a necessity for safety.

There are additional safety precautions for paddlers with disabilities. The question of how the student's disability will affect rescue plans must always be answered and the solutions practiced in advance. For example, if a paddler is unable to initiate self-rescue, a safety boat must be next to that paddler's boat at all times. The type of rescue that will be used must have been practiced with that paddler in a safe environment prior to paddling on the open water. Other specific cautions are noted in the "Disabilities and Implications" section.

# CHAPTER THREE

# The Instructor Checklist

The following is a checklist to be used by instructors in planning a class which includes students, able and disabled. Keep in mind, depending on the students abilities, that different teaching techniques and more class time may be needed. For example, more time may be needed between classes if fatigue is a problem for any of the students. A detailed discussion on each of these topics follows in the related sections in this manual.

1. Plan the location, consider the accessibility of the site.
2. Read Medical Information Sheets completed by all students.
3. Conduct a Paddler's Interview with each student.
   - Review completed Medical Information Sheet with the student.
   - Determine if disclosure of medical information to other class members is needed. If so, discuss disclosure with the student.
4. Assess the abilities of the paddler.
5. Decide on group or individual instruction.
6. Determine swimming ability.
7. Determine the best choice and size of the PFD.
8. Establish an appropriate instructor/student ratio.
9. Complete adaptations to equipment with the student before the first class.
10. Discuss appropriate clothing.

## ACCESSIBILITY

Before a student using a wheelchair, crutches, or walker comes for instruction, check the site. Do the parking lot, walkways, entrance, and interior doors have level surfaces and 36 inch passageways? Is there enough room inside the rest room and dressing rooms for a wheelchair to turn? A five-foot turning radius would be ideal. Could a student using a wheelchair reach the pool or waterfront without help? If there are problem areas, change what you can. Remember the areas that remain a problem and be sure to mention them to anyone using a wheelchair before she arrives, if possible. Forewarning is important.

Often the slope of the land is deceiving and a person in a wheelchair may have difficulty pushing or slowing her chair at that angle. The recommended maximum gradient is a 1 inch rise in 12 inches of length. If in doubt about the accessibility of a site, ask the advice of a person who uses a wheelchair prior to using the area.

There will be sites where the use of wheelchairs, walkers, crutches, etc. will be difficult. In these settings, carries may be needed.

## MEDICAL INFORMATION SHEET

A comprehensive general medical information sheet should be completed by **every student**, able and disabled, prior to instruction. We recommend a general, nondiscriminatory form be used with all students. A sample form is in Appendix 3. It is the responsibility of the student to disclose all pertinent information.

The medical information sheet must be returned to the instructor before the in-depth interview. The completed form gives the instructor a starting point for discussion of any physical disability. This discussion is part of the paddler's interview.

## PADDLER'S INTERVIEW

A private interview with each student, able or disabled, is necessary before the first instructional session. The purpose is to develop a mutual understanding of expectations and to estimate the student's ability level. This is also the time to discuss implications for paddling due to a disability and possible adaptations. Ability is the emphasis. Adaptations compensate for disability, but it is ability that brings success. If the student will be taking private instruction, this interview could be a part of the first lesson.

The use of the medical information sheet and a careful paddler's interview are keys to instructing students with disabilities.

The student must have confidence in you as her instructor. This confidence comes from a combination of respect for your ability and experience and from the understanding that you will listen to the student's concerns. The student is the expert on her disability; you are the expert on paddling. With teamwork you can do it. Explain this concept early in the interview. You don't need to know all the answers. You do need to be willing to learn from your student. Open and comfortable communication between the student and instructor is essential.

**Ask every student these key questions:**
- *What are her expectations?*
- *What type of paddling interests her? exercise, recreation, competition, etc.*
- *Does her ability match that type of paddling?*
- *Is she aware of other paddling options such as sea kayaking, river kayaking, or lake paddling?*

**With the student's completed medical information sheet in hand:**
- *Does she have any additional information to add?*
- *Is there any information that should be discussed?*

**With the student who has a physical disability:**
- *Admit it if you do not know about the disabling condition.*
- *Ask questions about the disability or management of symptoms.*

The student must understand that she is responsible for informing the instructor about the extent of her physical abilities and skills.

It is important to know how long the student has been disabled. Such information may help in understanding the student's emotional response during instruction. If the disability is more recent, there may be more frustration in new learning situations. Students who have been sheltered by family/friends may have unrealistic expectations. However, students whose disabilities are long-term are often more prepared to deal with the difficulties they may experience during instruction.

Explain you will use as much standard equipment as possible and adapt equipment only as needed. Is the student willing to give feedback on which adaptations are helpful and which are not? Each person is affected differently by her disability and adaptations must be developed accordingly. For example, if the student with arthritis discovers a certain paddle stroke is difficult due to the position of the hands, she should feel comfortable informing the instructor. Creative problem-solving is a team (instructor/student) responsibility.

With all students, the inherent risk factors must be thoroughly explained by the instructor and understood by the student. If the instructor has doubts about the experience or ability the student claims to have, the instructor should observe the student in an appropriate boat before placing her in a class that will require that skill level.

Should the student have group or private instruction? The answer is determined by her ability level which is based on:

- *Previous paddling experience*
- *Determination/willingness to work*
- *Physical ability once equipment is adapted.*

Group instruction is appropriate if her ability level will allow her to progress at an average or above average rate.

Private instruction is appropriate if her ability will not allow her to progress at an average rate or if she prefers private instruction.

If the instructor has doubts after this detailed interview that the student is not telling the whole truth, the instructor must thoroughly evaluate whether or not to take that student into a class.

## DISCLOSURE OF MEDICAL INFORMATION

Disclosure (explanation to others) must be discussed with the student, if her disability will affect others in any way. For example, within a class, if the student is hearing impaired and needs to see the mouth of the individual with whom she is speaking, that explanation will need to be made at the first session Does the student prefer to make the explanation, or would she prefer to have the instructor explain? If the instructor is asked to explain, be sure the details of the explanation meet with the student's approval before the explanation is made to the class.

Never disclose any medical information without the student's prior approval. If the instructor feels the student's disability may affect others in the group and the student is unwilling to permit disclosure, the instructor must decide if it is appropriate to accept that student in the class. Lack of such disclosure may cause confusion and frustration for other students in the group. For example:

On an extended wilderness trip, one of the participants had a disability which was not obvious but caused fatigue. She adamantly refused to allow the trip leaders to disclose her disability to the other participants. During the trip she paddled less than the others and did little of the camp work. The other participants perceived her as lazy and the trip leaders as showing favoritism. The other participants complained to the leaders, but the leaders, bound to their previous commitment to the paddler, could not discuss the paddler's disability. The paddler continued to refuse to agree to disclosure. As a result the group cohesion never developed and her lack of disclosure had a negative impact on the trip.

## WHAT CAN SHE DO?

Ability is both physical and mental - body and willpower. Thankfully, there is no formula by which to prejudge any student's ability level. Often people ask what will a person with a specific disability be able to do. For example, "Can a T-4 roll a boat?". (When referring to a spinal cord injury or disease the letter/number combination refers to the exact area of the spine where the injury occurred.) Appendix 2 gives a detailed description of spinal cord injuries.

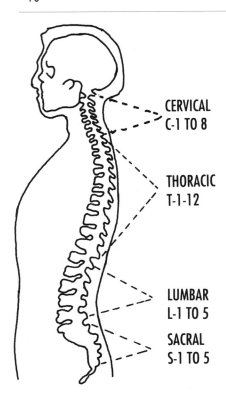

CERVICAL
C-1 TO 8

THORACIC
T-1-12

LUMBAR
L-1 TO 5

SACRAL
S-1 TO 5

Two students diagnosed at the same level of injury, e.g. (for example) T-4, may have different abilities. The level of injury does not, by itself, define the student's potential. One may have a complete injury and another incomplete. When uncertain about a student's ability to perform a certain technique, have her try it in a safe environment. Every disability affects the individual differently - physically and emotionally. The student's determination also affects her potential.

Determination plays a major role in success, positive or negative. For example, Eskimo rolling is a skill which requires repeated practice and may take more time for a student with a disability. If the person says, "Rolling is hard. I will never be able to do it," her negative attitude will influence the outcome.

## SWIMMING ABILITY

How well must a student be able to swim in order to qualify as a potential paddler? This is a tough question to answer. A sense of ease in the water is a necessity for every student.

Each person's situation will have to be considered. What is the person's ability with a properly-fitted personal flotation device (PFD)? The final decision regarding minimum swimming standards is a multifaceted one which requires careful and individual consideration.

Factors which may influence this decision include:
- Student's sense of ease in the water.
- Student's strength, fatigue level, and general conditioning.
- Instructor/student ratio.
- Type of PFD to be used.
- Paddling experience.
- Weather and water conditions.

Non-swimmers or weak swimmers who are able to float comfortably in their PFDs may be accepted as a student if other factors are satisfied. However, non-swimmers and weak swimmers should be strongly encouraged to take swimming classes. It is the decision of the instructor whether or not to take a weak swimmer into the class.

## RATIO OF INSTRUCTORS TO STUDENTS

Recommendations from canoeing and kayaking instructors working with students who have physical disabilities vary from a ratio of one to one to that of one to eight. In their whitewater clinics for students with disabilities, the Nantahala Outdoor Center uses a ratio of no more than two students with disabilities per instructor.

Considerations when determining ratio of instructors to students include:
- Skill level of students
- Environment (pool/river/lake/ocean)

For example, a pool session with students who have had some paddling experience will allow for more students per instructor than a lake setting with beginning students.

## ADAPTATIONS

The rule with adaptations is: use as much standard equipment as possible. Make appropriate adaptations to the equipment only as needed. When you plan to adapt equipment, have several possible adaptations in mind but wait to make them until you are with the student. The manual describes many possible adaptations. By trying the adaptations, the student can best tell you what is helpful and what is not. Adaptations must be completed with the student before the first instructional session. Successful adaptations may come quickly or they can be time-consuming. Often creative problem-solving between the instructor and the student with a disability is necessary. This time provides an excellent opportunity for the student and the instructor to become acquainted. The right adaptation can open up the world of paddling for that student. A result that is definitely worth the time!

## PLAN AHEAD

Planning is the key to all successful instruction. Make use of the tools the manual gives you. Incorporate these guidelines into your plans. Have the student fill out the Medical Information Sheet and hold a detailed Paddler's Interview. Use the section on Disabilities and their Implications for Paddling to gain information about the specific disability involved and the teaching suggestions will guide you. The rest of your plans will hinge on that information.

# CHAPTER FOUR

# Equipping the Paddler

## CLOTHING

Because many disabilities impair circulation, the effects of cold and heat are an increased concern. The greater the chance of immersion and the more severe the paddling conditions, the more protection is needed. Proper clothing should be worn to prevent hypothermia (a lowering of the body's core temperature that eventually can cause unconsciousness and death).

It is important to recognize the stages of hypothermia. Watch for its early signs such as shivering, muscle incoordination, skin numbness, and mild confusion. In paddlers with reduced or absent sensation in the extremities, skin numbness or shivering may be absent.

Hypothermia occurs most rapidly in a cold, wet, windy environment. Water temperature, reduced physical activity, clothing, body build, and the person's sex are all factors influencing survival in cold water. Consult general outdoor texts or emergency manuals for more detailed information on hypothermia if you are not familiar with the signs, symptoms, and treatment.

Care must be taken in selecting the clothing. The paddler needs clothing for two purposes: to repel wind and water and to insulate for heat retention. Recommended is a versatile layering system which features long underwear, insulation, and a shell. Layering allows a paddler to regulate her body temperature at a comfortable level through the addition or removal of layers. The intensity of exercise and air temperature changes affect this process.

Garments are available in many fabrics. Wool is the best natural fiber for providing warmth, although it is difficult to dry and can be irritating to sensitive skin. Garments made of fiberpile provide less protection from skin injury than wet suits, but they are more comfortable to wear.

Layering is ideal when the paddler is dry. A waterproof top layer is needed. If an article is waterproof and not breathable, there may be another complication, i.e. any perspiration will stay within the garment. (See illustrations following page.)

Waterproof breathable fabrics (Goretex®, Entrant®, Sympatex®, etc.) are available. These are designed to keep out the rain while allowing perspiration to escape. Clothing made of waterproof breathable fabrics cost roughly twice as much as quality waterproof garments. Many paddlers do not recommend the use of waterproof breathable fabrics in a salt water environment due to their loss of reliability in that setting. However, numerous paddlers rely exclusively on these fabrics.

When in the water, a barrier (wet suit or dry suit) is the only way to aid in heat retention although it is not a guarantee against heat loss.

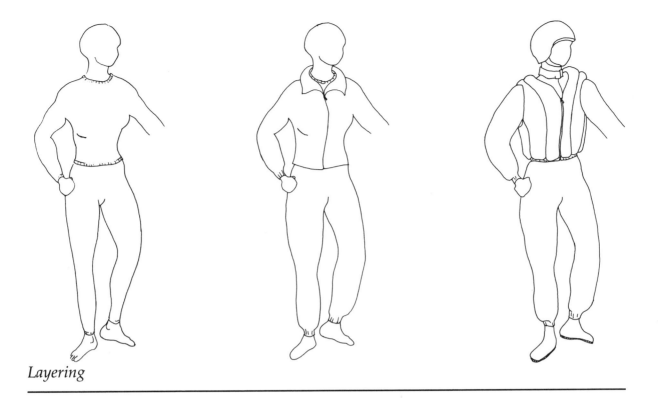

*Layering*

**Wet suits**, though difficult to get into, do have several benefits. They provide excellent padding and abrasion resistance for paddlers without sensitivity in their lower limbs. Very importantly, they also increase the buoyancy for student's legs in the event of a swim. Some wet suits have longer zippers down the chests and up the back of the calves for ease of access. It is also possible to add zippers to a wet suit.

Many instructors favor wet suit vests for some students with lower limb paralysis because the vests offer good torso insulation and are easier to put on than long john wet suits. A wet suit vest allows for unrestricted use of a catheter/leg bag. For the lower body, comfortable layers of capilene®, polypropylene, or wool covered with baggy paddling pants of waterproof nylon are a good combination.

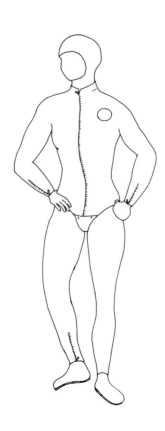

**Dry suits** are better at protecting sensitive skin from constant contact with water than wet suits. They keep all insulating layers worn underneath them almost completely dry. Dry suits are easier to put on, especially for some paddlers with lower limb disabilities, and they allow for unrestricted use of a catheter/leg bag. However, dry suits are more expensive than wet suits.

Keeping the head covered is a high priority because so much heat is lost through the head. Wool, polypropylene hats, or wet suit hoods are recommended. Not only is it important to keep the head covered in the cold, the head and neck can also be used to cool a person in the heat. Hats or bandanas can also be used to keep cool by wetting and wearing them.

Type III PFDs can supply a lot of insulation. Long-sleeved versions of Type III PFDs are also available. These are a cross between foul weather jackets and flotation gear. They do not look like PFDs; instead, they resemble all-purpose coats. These models need to be tried

while paddling to be sure that they will be comfortable without chafing.

Check the weather including the wind chill factor and water temperature. Many paddlers use the general formula that if the air temperature and the water temperature combined are less than 100°, wet suits or dry suits should be worn. However, this formula is misleading. For instance, the air temperature could be 80° and the water 54°. Using the formula, this combination of temperature would not require wet suits. However, if a paddler were immersed in 54°water the air temperature would not keep her warm. This formula would apply only if the wet paddler exited the water quickly and the air temperature warmed her up. It does not apply when a paddler may be immersed in cold water for more than twenty minutes.

Be prepared. The weather can change quickly. Bring along a change of clothes in a waterproof bag.

## PFDs / Life Jackets
Wear a U. S. Coast Guard approved personal flotation device (PFD) for adequate flotation, physical protection and warmth.

In choosing a PFD, proper fit and intended use must be considered. A PFD should fit snugly, but not be too tight. A loose oversized vest tends to ride up on the wearer, can interfere with her swimming, and can force her face into the water. Vests that are too small restrict movement. Side adjustment tabs at the waistband are helpful to allow for different layers of clothing. PFDs should be tried in the water at least once a season as they lose buoyancy over time.

**Type I.** This style provides the most flotation. Type I's will turn and float most unconscious people in a face-up position. A type I is recommended for people who are prone to seizures. This style is bulky and is not available in a wide range of sizes. This style is also called a "life jacket".

*Type I*

**Type II.** This "horsecollar" style is bulky, and as you move your arms while paddling, it tends to ride up around your ears in an irritating manner. All ties must be securely fastened, or it may slip off the paddler if she capsizes. This style does not provide adequate body protection or warmth and is not recommended for long hours in rough water.

*Type II*

**Type III.** This style is most commonly used by paddlers. It is a comfortable vest for continuous wear with a zipper in front, and closed-cell foam flotation sewn into narrow pockets or flat panels in the front and rear. The vertical flotation in this style may provide some torso support. Type III vests provide high buoyancy, warmth, support, and body protection from obstacles. This style will not turn and float an unconscious person in a face-up position. The vests are available in a variety of sizes and amounts of flotation. High-float vests, which offer higher levels of buoyancy, are recommended for people needing the extra flotation, e.g. swimmers needing assistance. The short style is recommended for use with a kayak and skirt and for short people.

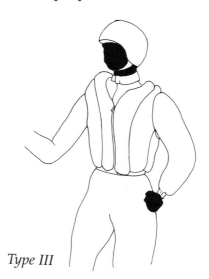

*Type III*

**Type IV.** This type is a boat cushion/throwable device, unsuitable for use as a paddler's PFD.

**Type V.** Included in this category is a hybrid inflatable device which requires inflation but is the least bulky PFD when uninflated. The wearer completes an inflation procedure and must protect the inflation chamber from damage. This PFD may not adequately float some wearers unless fully inflated. Inflate periodically to be sure it is working properly.

PFDs should be tried in a safe body of water, e.g. pool or calm shallow area, to allow the wearer to experience the support of the PFD and to give her confidence in its use. Try a variety of PFDs in the water, if possible, before buying.

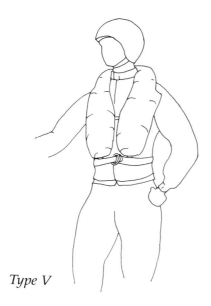

*Type V*

## CANOES AND KAYAKS

Stability, maneuverability, and weight vary with the different models of canoes and kayaks. Consider the paddler's needs. Weight and durability of the boat are two considerations for paddlers with disabilities. If a paddler lacks upper body strength, a lighter boat may be preferable. If she needs to drag her boat at the launch/landing site, a durable boat is her best choice.

Selecting a boat requires careful thought. Paddlers should try many styles of canoes, river kayaks, and sea kayaks before buying one. A student should consider renting first. She might complete her instruction before deciding which boat best meets her abilities and intended use. She should research boat and paddle styles through reading, talking to other paddlers, asking in canoe and kayak stores, and trying different boats in the water.

A **canoe** can be a solo ( single) or a tandem (double) boat and varies in length from 13 to 18 feet. Because a canoe is open, it offers the easiest entry and exit and access to gear. However, seating stability is more difficult to adapt in an open canoe. A single-bladed paddle is normally used. Tandem paddling is ideal if one paddler is unable to manage a solo canoe due to fatigue, level of disability, etc. (Illustration following page.)

A **decked canoe** is 12 to 13 feet long for one paddler (C-l) and 15 feet for two paddlers (C-2). These boats are designed to be maneuverable. A decked canoe is paddled from a kneeling position and a single-bladed paddle is used. Cockpit size varies and these boats do not have built-in storage areas. (Illustration following page.)

A **river kayak** is 10 to 13 feet long and built for maneuverability. The size of the cockpit varies with each model. Storage areas are not built into these kayaks, because they are not intended for tripping. They require a double-bladed paddle. Good sitting balance is necessary and may be obtained through appropriate adaptations. There is at least one double kayak, the Double Topolino by Prijon, which can be used on rivers. For a paddler who is visually impaired, or is easily fatigued, a tandem boat could be used. (Illustration following page.)

An individual with lower-limb disabilities interested in whitewater kayaking should chose a stable, flatter-bottomed kayak that is wider than average. The size of the cockpit should be taken into consideration for ease in entering and safety in exiting.

For canoes and river kayaks, instruction involves paddling, safety and rescue techniques, and water reading skills.

A **sea kayak** is 15 to 20 feet long and built for stability, tracking (going straight), and speed over long distances. Paddlers use a double-

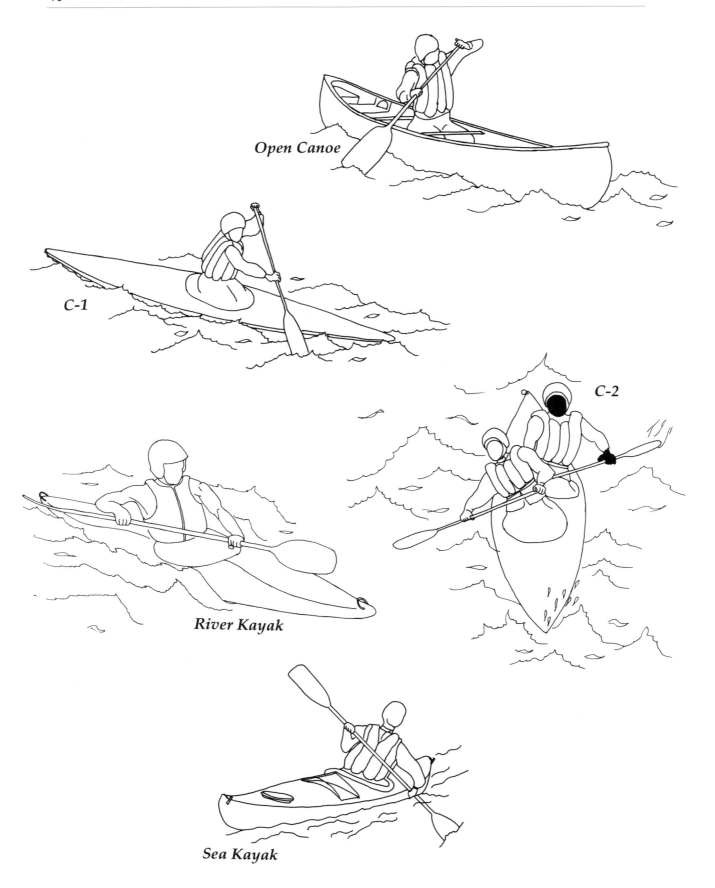

Open Canoe

C-1

C-2

River Kayak

Sea Kayak

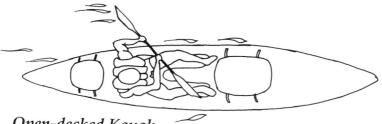

*Open-decked Kayak*

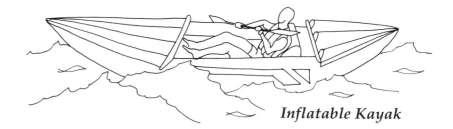

*Inflatable Kayak*

bladed paddle. The cockpit area or opening tends to be larger than that of a river kayak, and storage areas to carry gear are built-in. A number of British sea kayaks have small cockpits. A tandem sea kayak is ideal if one paddler is not able to manage a solo kayak due to fatigue or level of disability.

Coastal kayaking (open water paddling) instruction involves paddling, launching and landing techniques, safety and rescue techniques, tides, navigation, etc.

Also available:

**Open-decked kayaks** resemble surfboards with a place on the top deck in which to sit. They are easier to get into and out of than closed boats. They do not offer protection from the cold, and seating adaptations for students with balance problems can be difficult. Some instructors like using these boats as a rescue craft on outings because it is easy to exit the boat to assist a capsized paddler. It is also easier to get a capsized paddler onto this boat during a rescue than into a decked kayak or into a canoe.

**Inflatable kayaks** come in self-bailing models with inflated floors that are well padded. The boats can be adapted with rubber and/or Hypalon® glue-on patches to which padding can be clipped, taped, or attached with Velcro®. Adapting the seating for students with balance problems may be difficult.

## PADDLES

Paddles are available in a variety of lengths, weights, materials, blade shapes, and blade angles. A canoeist uses a single-bladed paddle; river kayakers use a shorter double-bladed paddle than those used by sea kayakers. Double-bladed paddles have flat or spoon-shaped blades. On double-bladed paddles, offset blades are called "feathered"; parallel blades are called "unfeathered."

Good paddling techniques will increase the efficiency of the stroke. Torso rotation should be used by those who can master these techniques; it makes use of the large muscle groups, increases the efficiency of the stroke, and is less tiring. Paddlers with disabilities should choose a paddle that will help them compensate.

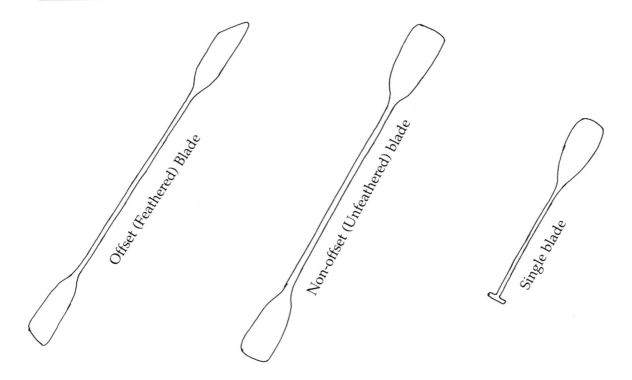

### Length
A longer paddle provides:
- More stability in bracing strokes for paddlers with decreased sitting balance.
- More efficient turning strokes for paddlers with less strength.
- An extended reach for paddlers with limited range of motion.
- An extended reach for paddlers with seat lowered for greater stability.
- An extended reach for paddlers with limited use of their arms.

**Note**: A kayak paddle should not be longer than 220 cm. because a longer length becomes unwieldy and cancels out the advantage of greater leverage.

### Weight/Materials
A lighter paddle requires less effort for:
- Paddlers with decreased strength and/or who fatigue easily.

### Blade Shapes
A smaller blade area requires less effort and wind resistance for:

- Paddlers with decreased strength and/or who fatigue easily.
- Paddlers with hand/wrist disabilities.

### Blade Angles
Unfeathered blades on double-bladed paddles require less wrist rotation for:
- Paddlers with hand/wrist disabilities.
- Paddlers with decreased strength and/or who fatigue easily.
- Paddlers with decreased sitting balance will gain increased stability with bracing strokes.

**Note:** Some take-apart paddles give the paddler the option to feather or unfeather the blade angle. Some take-aparts allow three different adjustments for left-hand control, right-hand control, or unfeathered.

Use unfeathered double-bladed paddles in open canoes for:
- Paddlers with limited range of motion.
- Better bracing since there is a blade on both sides.
- Paddlers with limited use of their arms.

- Paddlers who need extensive hand adaptations since the grip of the top hand on a single-bladed paddle is harder to adapt.

When a person is weaker on one side than the other, the hand placement may be changed on double-bladed paddles. The paddler could move her hands closer to the blade on her stronger side. This strategy keeps the boat tracking well because the stroke on the weaker side is now farther from the center of the boat and turns the boat back onto a straight course. The change in hand placement compensates for the over-correcting effect of the stronger side.

## ACCESSORIES

**Helmets** are worn by river kayakers, canoeists in decked boats, and some open boat paddlers.

**Air bags** in canoes and kayaks are necessary equipment. Air bags provide additional flotation and displace water in the event of a capsize. A canoe/kayak with less water is much lighter to rescue. Some styles of air bags provide waterproof storage areas.

**Bulkheads** are used in some kayaks to separate the cockpit area from the rest of the boat. These serve the same purpose as air bags and provide deck and boat support. They can be placed strategically in the boat to serve as foot braces in place of foot pegs. The advantage to using bulkheads for a foot rest is that there is no danger of foot entrapment for a paddler who has no control of her legs in a wet exit.

**Sea socks** are designed for use with sea kayaks without bulkheads or as a backup to those with leaky bulkheads. The sea sock provides an acceptable method of limiting the amount of water which can enter the kayak in the event of capsize. One sea kayak, the Puffin by Nimbus, has a built-in pod which completely separates the area where the paddler sits from the rest of the boat.

A **boat cart**, a wheeled device which folds or comes apart, is used to aid in moving a canoe or kayak on land. Varied in style and load capacities, they are available through canoe/ kayak dealers and sporting goods stores.

**Slings** can be used for boat storage. Loading and unloading from the vehicle can be made easier by using a pulley system with the slings.

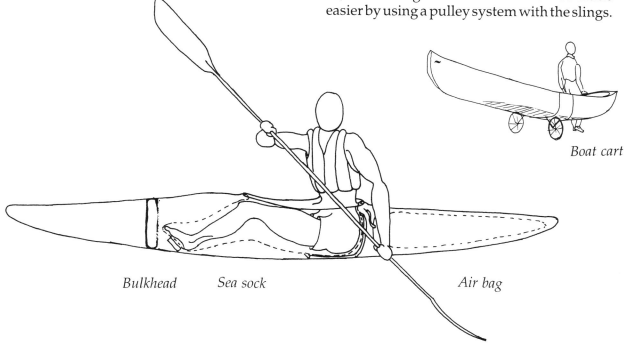

*Boat cart*

*Bulkhead*        *Sea sock*                    *Air bag*

# CHAPTER FIVE

# Disabilities, Implications for Paddling, and Teaching Suggestions

The purpose of this section is to provide a brief overview of various disabilities, the *possible* effect(s) on paddling, and teaching suggestions. Although every effort has been made to make this as comprehensive as possible, it is neither possible nor practical to cover all disabling conditions or diseases. Each person must be considered individually regardless of the particular disability because every individual is affected differently by her disability. For example, one person with multiple sclerosis may have minimal physical disabilities, and another person with the same disease may be unable to walk or sit unsupported. For this reason, this section will describe the various disabilities in functional terms rather than medical terms as much as possible. A glossary is provided in Appendix 1 to clarify medical terms which are used in the descriptions.

A person may have a combination of functional impairments. For example, a person with quadriplegia may have involvement of arms, hands, legs, feet and trunk. Read the information under each related functional impairment.

The following are considerations for **all** paddlers and are not restated in the various teaching suggestions:

- Teach paddling technique which uses torso rotation. This method makes use of the large muscle groups, increases the efficiency of the stroke, and is less tiring.
- Encourage general paddling conditioning.
- Allow ample time for rest and set the pace of the trip appropriately.
- Dehydration reduces one's capacity to maintain top fitness, so fluid intake is an important factor in reducing fatigue.
- Wear proper clothing.
- Bracing strokes and Eskimo rolls are important to know to avoid unnecessary swims.

## Functional Impairment:

■ *Right and/or Left Upper Limb(s) (Arm/ Hand).e.g. arthritis, cerebral palsy, hemiplegia, quadriplegia, multiple sclerosis, etc.*

## *Possible* Implications for Paddling Teaching Suggestions and Adaptations

### Difficulty in holding paddle

- Use adapted grip on paddle. (Adapted equipment, p. and paddle description, p. 19, 46)

### Lack of strength

- Try a double-bladed paddle.
- Keep the paddle low to the boat while paddling.
- A paddler with reduced function in the triceps can pull the paddle even though pushing with the opposite hand may be difficult.
- Teach the paddler to pull the blade slowly as it is easier to paddle slowly because less turbulence is created.

### Lack of control of paddle movements, e.g. tremor

- Weighted wrist cuffs and/or heavier paddles may help to decrease hand tremor but it also increases the effort required to move the paddle.
- Consider using either a right-hand or left-hand controlled double-bladed paddle depending on which side is stronger and has more control.

### Range of motion affected

- Consider using an unfeathered kayak paddle or a 70° blade angle instead of a 90°. Reducing the blade angle requires less wrist torque.
- A paddle with a smaller blade area for either canoeing or kayaking could be used because a large blade area requires more strength to use.

### Swimming ability affected

- The instructor should thoroughly evaluate swimming ability and possibly

## Functional Impairment:

## *Possible* Implications for Paddling Teaching Suggestions and Adaptations

recommend higher flotation PFD or a Type I device. (PFD, p.15)
- Recommend that the student take an adapted aquatics class, if possible, before beginning instruction.

### Easily fatigued
- Consider using lighter weight paddle and lighter boat.

### Difficulty entering and exiting the boat
- Be ready to provide additional support to compensate for loss of balance.
- Practice wet exits in a pool.

### Difficulty carrying the boat
- Use boat carrying carts and scout for an easy put-in or launching site which does not require as much carrying.

### Susceptibility to cold/heat
- Prepare for different weather and water conditions by using proper clothing. (Clothing, p.13)

■ *Upper Limb(s) Amputations*

### With high amputations, one may have difficulty with the fit of the PFD and keeping the PFD on when swimming.
- Use crotch-type fastenings or crotch straps on PFD to ensure that it fits properly and doesn't ride up or slip off over the head. Consider using a PFD with an adjustable waistband or a shortie style which does not ride up when sitting.

### Prosthesis may be damaged or fill up with water.
- Balance and swimming ability may be affected by waterlogged prosthesis. Keep the prosthesis in a waterproof container

## Functional Impairment:

### Possible Implications for Paddling
### Teaching Suggestions and Adaptations

*Upper Limb(s) Amputations*
*cont.*

attached to boat or use a prosthesis designed for use in water.

### Limb prone to injury if unprotected
- Wear a protective device over the exposed stump.

### Difficulty in holding the paddle
- In the bow of a canoe, the paddler could hold a single-bladed paddle under her stump. The stern paddler could use a double-bladed paddle to compensate. (Adaptations, p. 50)
- Use an adapted style of paddle.
- Modifications need to be made to either the waterproof prosthesis or the paddle to allow adequate grip on the paddle, e.g. attachment system to paddle. Must be tested in safe environment first. (Adaptations,p. 50)

■ *Neck and/or trunk. e.g. cerebral palsy, paraplegia, quadriplegia (affecting trunk balance), etc.*

### Difficulty sitting unsupported
- Seat needs to be modified.(Adaptations, p.54)
- Back support is a must and support at the sides of the paddler's chest may also be needed.
- Always allow for easy exit from the boat.
- Avoid chest straps.

### Difficulty in performing some strokes
- Teach a variety of strokes.
- Try a double-bladed paddle in a canoe as the grip may be easier to adapt for certain hand disabilities than the shaft of a canoe paddle.
- Try an adaptation for the paddle. (Adaptations, p. 46)

## Functional Impairment:

## *Possible* Implications for Paddling Teaching Suggestions and Adaptations

### *Balance affected; balance affects lean or trim of the boat*

- Seat needs to be modified.(Adaptations, p. 54)
- In a canoe, lowering the seat one to four inches may be helpful to improve balance; however sitting on the bottom of the canoe decreases stroke efficiency.
- In a kayak, add enough padding on the seat to protect against pressure sores, but keep in mind that a higher center of gravity reduces stability.
- Paddler must have her weight distributed evenly (boat trim) so boat direction is not affected. The paddler may not be aware that her weight has shifted to one side. Paddling companions can watch for uneven weight distribution.
- Paddle a tandem kayak or canoe so partner can help with balance.
- Bracing strokes are essential to learn.
  - Practice braces with the paddle being supported by an instructor.
  - Bracing strokes can also be practiced with a paddle float on the end of the blade in the water.
  - In a pool, lines can be tied to the bow and stern of the student's boat and the boat can be towed along the pool to give the sense of using both high or low braces while the boat is moving.

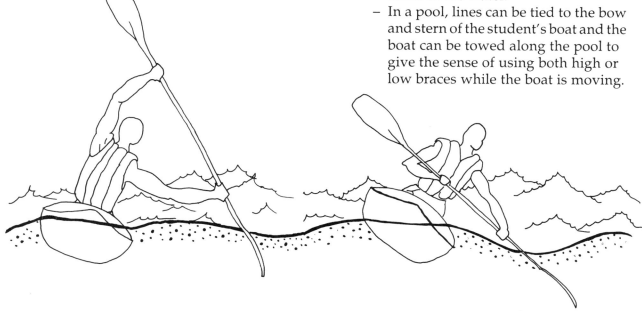

## Functional Impairment:

*Neck and/or trunk e.g. cerebral palsy, paraplegia, quadriplegia (affecting trunk balance), etc.*
*cont.*

## *Possible* Implications for Paddling Teaching Suggestions and Adaptations

- Video taping is a helpful instructional tool to show the paddler how she is leaning in her boat as well as her general technique.

### *More susceptible to temperature variations*
- Use proper clothing. (Clothing, p. 13)

### *Difficulty entering and exiting the boat*
- Practice wet exits.
- Be ready to provide support for balance.
- Mount grab handles on the boat to help the paddler pull herself into the boat. (Adaptations, p. 53)

■ *Right and/or Left Lower Limb(s) (leg/foot), individuals using wheelchairs e.g. amputation, hemiplegia, paraplegia, muscular dystrophy, etc.*

### *Difficulty entering and exiting the boat*
It is generally easier to transfer from a wheelchair to/from the boat (kayak/canoe) on shore rather than when the boat is floating because the height of the seats is more equal.

- Mount grab handles on the boat to help the paddler pull herself into the boat. (Adaptation, p. 53)
- If it is necessary to transfer from a dock/pool deck to the floating boat, a person may be able to transfer from her wheelchair directly to the dock/pool deck and then into her boat which must be held stably.
- When the boat is stable at the water's edge, a person may be able to place her wheelchair next to the boat and transfer from her wheelchair to the boat.
- A mid-point transfer may be helpful. Place a cooler or overturned milk crate between the wheelchair and the boat. Pad the top with a towel. Transfer from the wheelchair to the mid-point, then to the boat. Reverse the transfer process when exiting the boat. By breaking the transfer into two parts, the total height

## Functional Impairment:

## *Possible* Implications for Paddling
## Teaching Suggestions and Adaptations

of each transfer is more manageable.
- When the boat is on the dock/land a person could transfer into the boat and then the boat and paddler can be placed in the water.

Individuals know the best way to transfer themselves. The instructor discusses the transfer with the student then uses this information to determine the safest place to complete the transfer. Ask for direction from the student and offer assistance. An example is, *"I am willing to help. Tell me what to do if you want my help."* If she agrees to assistance, ask where you should place your hands. Individuals unable to transfer independently can direct others as to the amount and type of assistance required. Take care not to injure yourself, especially your back, during this process. When lifting, always bend at the knees and keep the lower back straight, using leg strength, not back strength.

### *Paddler may have special appliances*
*e.g. catheter/leg bag or colostomy appliance*
- Care must be taken when transferring from a wheelchair to a boat to make sure that these appliances are not moved out of place. The individual can give instruction as to hand placement, etc. to assist with the transfer.

### *Difficulty in sitting stably*
Sliding in the boat seat while paddling affects balance and makes paddle strokes less effective.
- Person should be secure in the seat but still allow for a free exit. Adaptations may need to be made to the seat and the area around the seat. (Adaptations, p. 54)
- An upward angle at the front edge of the seat will aid in preventing the paddler from sliding forward in her seat. (Adaptations, p. 58)

## Functional Impairment:

*Right and/or Left Lower Limb(s) (leg/foot), individuals using wheelchairs e.g. amputation, hemiplegia, paraplegia, muscular dystrophy, etc.*
*cont.*

## *Possible* Implications for Paddling Teaching Suggestions and Adaptations

- A stump holder can be built into the craft to protect the stump and to prevent the person from sliding.
- Legs need to be placed evenly in the boat. Often when the boat leans, the leg on the high side may shift to the low side and affect balance.
- Padding can be designed and placed between the legs to keep them separated. Be sure that this padding does not hinder exits.
- Seat belts such as a quick release belt may be used. Precautions have to be taken.(Seat belts, p. 70) Pre-test safety belt in a controlled setting e.g., pool to make sure it works properly. Airplane seatbelts or jet ski belts are recommended plus a backup release system such as a Velcro® attachment to the seat. (Adaptations, p. 62)

### *Difficulty in maintaining balance of the boat*
- Compensate for weight loss in lower limbs due to amputation or decrease in muscle mass by adding ballast to the boat. (Adaptations, p. 63)

### *Concern for wheelchair security*
- Paddler may be concerned about the security of her chair when it is left on the shore. She may want the chair brought along if the group will be landing somewhere during the paddle.
- Wheelchair should be placed in a secure location; locked in a vehicle is best. Be sure other people will not sit in it, play with it, etc. It should be brought with the group if another land location is used. If it is a manual, folding wheelchair it can be brought in a canoe. A battery-powered wheelchair would need to be transported in a vehicle.

## Functional Impairment:

## *Possible* Implications for Paddling Teaching Suggestions and Adaptations

### *Difficulty exiting from a boat in the event of a capsize*

- Remove the foot pegs from a kayak to avoid foot entrapment or injury.
- In a canoe, do not place the paddler's legs under a thwart where they may be pinned in a capsize.
- When using seating adaptations, check for easy exit.

### *Decreased sensation and circulation/prone to bruising and skin abrasion*

- Pad with closed-cell foam to protect any areas where skin without sensation will come in contact with the boat. Without sensation, the paddler may be unaware that she is being injured. (Mini-cell blue foam does not break down in ultraviolet light.)
- Padding on the bottom of a kayak will also help insulate the legs from the water cooling the boat bottom.
- Too much padding affects the boat's balance because it raises the paddler's center of gravity.
- Foot protection and long pants should be worn.
- The paddler may need to check appropriate areas for pressure points caused by prolonged sitting in one position without adequate cushioning.
- For paddlers who are susceptible to skin breakdown, it is important to keep the skin as dry as possible.
- Care must be taken not to cause bruises when helping with transfer from a wheelchair to the boat.
- Care must be taken to avoid having sensitive skin stay wet for a long period of time as skin may breakdown more quickly when wet.

## Functional Impairment:

*Right and/or Left Lower Limb(s) (leg/foot), individuals using wheelchairs e.g. amputation, hemiplegia, paraplegia, muscular dystrophy, etc.*
*cont.*

## *Possible* Implications for Paddling
## Teaching Suggestions and Adaptations

### *Increased susceptibility to temperature variations.*

- With a spinal cord injury or disease, the body's temperature control may be disrupted. Hypothermia and heat exhaustion may occur more quickly. Shivering and sweating may be absent so increased awareness is needed.
- Check the weather and water temperatures. Plan for temperature extremes (hot or cold).Remember the weather may change, the wind may rise, a storm may move in, etc. during the day. Be prepared.
- Clothing : Use dry suits, wet suits, polypropylene, or wool. Wearing a vest instead of a farmer-john-style wet suit is recommended as the latter is difficult to get on and may constrict a catheter/leg bag. Instead use wet suit booties and a layering system on the legs. Prepare for a variety of possible water and wind temperatures.
- Layering is helpful when the paddler is dry. A barrier (wet suit or dry suit) is the only system which will aid in retaining body heat when the paddler is in the water. One or two dry changes of clothes must be brought along for the group. (Clothing, p. 13)
- In handling anyone with hypothermia, one must be extremely gentle. Rewarming should be done slowly. Consult general outdoor texts or emergency manuals for more detailed information on hypothermia if you are not familiar with signs, symptoms, and treatment.
- Warm areas with normal sensation first and slowly. For example, in warming a person with a lack of sensation in her legs, warm the torso first. If a person

## Functional Impairment:

## *Possible* Implications for Paddling Teaching Suggestions and Adaptations

lacks sensation on one side of her body, first warm the side of the body which has normal sensation.

*Caution: In paddlers with no sensation, care must be taken not to expose the skin to extreme warmth because the paddler could be burned without feeling the heat. If skin is fragile, extremes in temperature against the skin will be harmful.*

### Sudden spasms affect balance

- Cold water, overexertion, sudden motion, and improper seating may cause an increase in spasticity.(Appendix 1) Avoid these causes if possible.

### Legs may drag or float due to a loss of muscle mass

- Ask the student if her legs tend to drag when in the water. On rivers it may be safer for her to float rapids on her back with her body sideways to the river. This position helps to prevent her legs/feet from becoming entangled, but it leaves the swimmer at great risk because she has no buffer between rocks, etc. and her head. A paddler should always practice swimming rapids in controlled conditions.
- It is always preferable to swim rapids feet first. A wet suit or a ring of Ethafoam® secured at the ankles will help her legs float and would allow her to swim in the safer feet first position. Such precautions must be taken before they are needed.

## Functional Impairment:

## *Possible* Implications for Paddling
## Teaching Suggestions and Adaptations

■ *General Impairment of Leg(s)*
*e.g. arthritis, phlebitis, etc.*

### Difficulty in kneeling in the canoe or sitting in a canoe or kayak

- Provide a seat support system to maximize stability.(Adaptations, p. 54)
- Consider lowering the seat slightly to lower the center of gravity and/or add back and side supports.

### Decreased sensation and circulation/prone to bruising and skin abrasion

- Provide seating with adequate cushioning.
- The instructor should be alert to the risk of hypothermia or heat exhaustion.
- Proper clothing should be worn. (Clothing, p.13)
- If circulation is decreased, do not kneel as that would further impair circulation.
- Check the inside of the boat for sharp or rough areas. Remove or pad those areas. If not possible protect the skin with proper padding or clothing.

■ *Lower Limb(s) Amputations*

### Difficulty entering and exiting the boat

- May require assistance getting into and out of the boat.
- Mount grab handles on the boat to help the paddler pull herself into the boat. (Adaptations, p. 53)

### Difficulty in sitting stably

- Person must be secure in the seat and still allow for free exit. (Adaptations, p. 63)
- A stump holder can be built into the craft to protect the stump and to prevent the person from sliding in the seat. The holder can be made using Ethafoam® covered with neoprene, closed-cell foam, or a similar material.

## Functional Impairment:

## *Possible* Implications for Paddling Teaching Suggestions and Adaptations

- Compensate for lower limb weight loss by adding ballast to the boat. (Adaptations, p. 63)

### Water (especially salt water) may damage the prosthesis

- Bring the prosthesis along to use when on land; however, it needs to be protected while in the boat. A waterproof container must be used and the prosthesis tied to the boat.

### Swimming ability is affected by the absence of a limb

- PFD must provide adequate flotation and fit securely.
- Student should first try swimming with PFD in a safe environment.

### If the prosthesis is worn, it may become waterlogged in a capsize

- Balance and swimming ability may be negatively affected. Explain this risk to the paddler.

■ *Hearing Impairment*

### Difficulty with on-water communication

- Practice signals to be used with all participants before they are needed.
- Simple signals are best. (On-water communication, p. 81)
- A bright orange flag could be used.
- Other paddlers must be observant as the person may not be able to hear an emergency whistle.
- Keep the same paddling partners together to facilitate development of signs and other communication techniques. Choose a paddling partner who is easy to lip read and who enunciates clearly.

## Functional Impairment:

## *Possible* Implications for Paddling Teaching Suggestions and Adaptations

*Hearing Impairment cont.*

### *Difficulty hearing the instructions or unable to hear them at all*

- Speak and look directly at the person.
- Speak clearly and distinctly, using normal tones. Shouting makes it harder to lip read.
- Mustaches may hinder lip reading.
- Make sure the person has visual contact with the instructor during instructional sessions.
- Demonstrations are valuable. If possible, begin instruction in a controlled situation (e.g. pool deck or pool), so that the instructor can stand behind the student or in the pool and physically manipulate the student's paddle.
- Be sure the sun is not at the speaker's back.
- Use pen and paper to facilitate communication, if necessary. Special pens are available from camping goods stores to be used when wet or use "wipe-off" communication boards (such as those used in scuba).
- Drawing directions in the sand can be done to explain the intended route.
- If a person who is hearing impaired is with an interpreter, direct your conversation to the person and not to the interpreter. (For example, say "Hold the paddle at this angle" rather than "Tell her to hold the paddle at this angle.")
- Check to be sure the instructions were understood by asking a direct question which requires an answer that summarizes the instruction.
- Person with a hearing impairment should not be in the bow or lead boat.
- When paddling tandem, tapping on the side of the canoe so the paddler with the hearing impairment can feel vibration is a good method to get her attention.

## Functional Impairment:

## *Possible* Implications for Paddling Teaching Suggestions and Adaptations

### *Balance may be affected*
- Lower the student's center of gravity in the boat, e.g. lower the seat, or suggest kneeling in a canoe instead of sitting.

### *Hearing aid and batteries may be damaged by water*
- Student must be informed of the risk to her equipment.
- Waterproof hearing aids are available. (Adaptations, p. 65)
- Consider carrying an extra hearing aid and batteries in a waterproof bag.

### *Difficulty in communicating during rescues*
- Practice rescues in a safe environment before going on the open water.
- Student should use a U. S. Coast Guard whistle in an emergency even if she cannot hear it. Try a loud, high-pitched U. S. Coast Guard whistle during rescue practice as a person who is hearing impaired may be able to hear it.

### ■ *Visual Impairment*

*Ask the student, " What can you see?"*

### *Difficulty following outlined course, e.g. sighting*
- Consider pairing the individual with a person who is not visually impaired so that person can give verbal instructions and can describe the physical environment, e.g. bend in the river, *spotting river trolls*, etc.
- Directions such as right/left or port/starboard work well with some individuals.
- Suggest using another stroke. In tandem boats, the paddler who has normal sight could say to her partner to draw harder or forward sweep. A simple word such as "change" could mean to change paddling sides.

## Functional Impairment:

## *Possible* Implications for Paddling Teaching Suggestions and Adaptations

*Visual Impairment*
*cont.*

### *Difficulty benefiting fully from visual demonstration*

- When teaching a person with a visual impairment in a group situation, use names so the person is aware she is being addressed.
- The instructor must give explicit, clear verbal instructions.
- After explaining to the student what you are going to do, hold the student's hands on the paddle to demonstrate strokes.
- When appropriate, try to make use of residual vision or memories of visual images. Try to make comparisons between the strokes and familiar actions. For instance, the pushing and pulling motions used when sweeping the floor can be compared to the arm motions used in the forward stroke.
- Use the clock method for directions (straight in front of the person is 12:00 and directly behind is 6:00). For instance, an instructor could tell the student to put in a stationary draw in the water at the same place as the 2 on a clock.
- Use tactile models. A small model river can be constructed on the floor using lines for the river banks, small rocks and a scale model canoe or kayak. The student can feel the curve of the shoreline as you explain the area of stronger currents on a curve, ferrying, the development of eddies around the rocks, etc. Tactile models are visually helpful for other students as well.
- Check to be sure instructions were understood.
- Try to avoid chatter as it tends to be distracting.

## Functional Impairment:

## *Possible* Implications for Paddling
## Teaching Suggestions and Adaptations

### *Difficulty with on-water communication*
- Practice signals with all participants before they are needed.
- A clanging device can be used for various signals, e.g. to gather for lunch, etc.
- A whistle should only be used for emergencies.

### *Difficulty in seeing boats during a rescue*
- Practice rescues before going on the open water.
- In whitewater, practice determining the current by feeling the water. This can be done with a hand, arm, or paddle placed in the water or by wading into the water. The paddler must understand water currents in order to not get confused. Water in eddies moves upstream. She should feel the current in several places around her to determine the main current.
- Practice swimming rapids with a buddy in safe areas.

### *Difficulty in knowing the location of the paddle blade*
- Tape a matchstick in line with the blade edge on the paddle shaft near the paddler's thumb. The paddler can quickly tell the blade angle by checking the location of the matchstick.

### *Must wear glasses/contacts to see clearly*
- Wear eyeglass holders (Chubs®, Croakies®, etc.). Bring extra glasses or contacts in a secure container.

### *Difficulty in determining which stroke to use*
- In tandem boats the paddler who has normal vision could tell her partner to draw or draw harder or forward sweep. etc. A simple word such as change could mean to change paddling sides.

## Functional Impairment:

*Lung Diseases e.g. asthma, emphysema, or any neurological or muscular disorder impairing the respiratory muscles*

## *Possible* Implications for Paddling Teaching Suggestions and Adaptations

### Shortness of breath and wheezing

- Shortness of breath may be brought on by overexertion, stress, high altitude, air temperature, or air quality. It is important to be aware of these causes and be alert to them. High pollen counts can irritate bronchial tubes and can exacerbate an asthma attack.
- Person with chronic breathing impairments may have an inhaler or other medicine that she uses. Keep extra inhaler or medicine handy and stored in a waterproof container which is tied to the boat.
- Watch for signs of labored breathing and encourage the person to rest before continuing.
- Supplemental breathing equipment including oxygen tanks can easily be carried in an open canoe. Breathing equipment should be secured in the canoe to avoid shifting of the weight in the bottom of the boat or in case of a capsize.

### Easily fatigued

- Watch for signs of fatigue and set the pace of the trip accordingly.
- Consider pairing the paddler with a strong partner.
- Rest after an attack until the person is ready to continue.

### Swimming may be affected

- Check swimming ability. Consider using Type I or more buoyant PFD. (PFD, p. 15)

### May be unable to assist in rescue

- Practice rescues.

## Functional Impairment:

## *Possible* Implications for Paddling
## Teaching Suggestions and Adaptations

*Side Effects of Medication*

*Check with the student during the Paddler's Interview about the side effects of any medicine if they are not listed on the Medical Information Sheet.*

### *Body temperature and its regulating mechanisms may be affected*

- Check weather and water temperatures. Proper clothing should be worn. (Clothing, p. 13)

### *Many psychotropic medicines cause severe dehydration*

- Fluid intake must be increased.

### *Increased sensitivity to the sunlight*

- Some drugs, such as phenothiazines, bactrim®, tetracycline®, psychotropic medicines, and others will result in hypersensitivity to the sun and individuals taking these drugs will burn easily. It is essential that the student be aware if her medication increases sun sensitivity. She should check with her physician or pharmacist.

*Caution: People who are allergic to sulfa drugs may react to sunscreens with the ingredient Paba® in them.*

### *Reflection is heightened on the water*

- Use sunvisors, sunblock or zinc oxide.
- Apply waterproof sunscreen with a minimum protection of #15 on all exposed parts of the body. The following is an easy to use formula for determining the amount of time that a particular sunscreen will protect a person. It is important to remember that this is a general guide and there will always be individual variations. If a person burns in the sun in 10 minutes and uses a #30 sunscreen, multiply the amount of time in minutes x the number on the sunscreen. In this case 10 x 30= 300. This person would be protected for 300 minutes or 5 hours.
- Apply sunblock to all exposed skin.

## Functional Impairment:

## *Possible* Implications for Paddling Teaching Suggestions and Adaptations

*Side Effects of Medication cont.*

- Reapply sunscreen after getting wet or splashing.
- Wear white or light-colored clothing.
- Hats with wide brims may be worn to protect the face from the sun. These may hold heat and should not be used if the person is very sensitive to the heat.
- Bandanas or scarves may be worn around the neck.
- Lightweight long-sleeved shirts and long pants also provide protection.
- Avoid paddling, if possible, during the prime sun hours of noon to four.

■ *Mental Impairment*

### *Requires more supervision than physically disabled*

- A suggested ratio of instructors to students is one to one.
- Instructor/student tandem paddling works well.

### *Will take more time to learn basic skills*

- Teach at a slow pace.
- Consider having separate classes as the pace is different.
- Practical demonstration is the main teaching aid, e.g. while holding onto the person's hands move the paddle through the stroke.
- Demonstrate the skill by breaking it into small parts.
- Make sure that each skill can be demonstrated before moving on to a new one.
- Will require frequent practices.
- It is essential that she gets the strokes and other important techniques correct the first time to avoid having to unlearn and relearn the information.
- Repeat the demonstration as many times as needed.
- Teach one or two strokes at first.
- Build on previous skills.

| **Functional Impairment:** | ***Possible* Implications for Paddling Teaching Suggestions and Adaptations** |

- Check to be sure that the instructions were understood by asking a direct question which requires an answer that summarizes the instruction.
- Proper supervision of the students is necessary.
- Give praise and encouragement as the students may be unable to judge their success.
- Include in the lesson only information that is necessary such as how to enter and exit the boat. Nothing will be gained by lengthy discussions on boat types or principles of paddling. Keep the lesson concrete and practical.
- Think of mnemonics or ways to help the person remember important points. For example, *"When in <u>doubt</u>, stop and <u>scout</u>."* or *"When there is an emergency, wave your paddle for all to see."*

### Difficulty in transferring the skill learned in one situation to a new situation

- Try not to make changes such as using a different boat or paddle or teaching in a different place because the person may become confused.

### Person may not complain about discomfort, thirst, fatigue, etc.

- Be aware to watch for problems such as these. Remind the person to drink liquids often.

### Difficulty realizing potential dangers

- Use a buddy system - an experienced paddler with a new student.

# CHAPTER SIX

# Adaptations

By simply changing the style of boat or paddle, the person with a disability may solve a boating problem she was having without needing to make equipment adaptations. (Equipment description, p. 13)

Use as much standard equipment as possible; adapt only as needed. Keep in mind that the more complicated a system, the more likely something will go wrong. All adaptations need to be tried in a safe setting before using them on an open body of water.

In developing adaptations one must first consider whether the adaptation is going to be temporary or permanent. For most beginning students with no equipment, adaptations will most likely be temporary. Use easily removed adaptations, e.g. duct tape and Ethafoam®, mini-cell foam, etc. which are closed-cell foams that do not absorb water. A club, camp, or facility which owns equipment may want to permanently adapt one or two canoes/kayaks with seating modifications, e.g. back support for those people with poor sitting balance. Several hand adaptations for paddles and a tie-on crotch strap for PFD modification could be available.

For adaptations which have been developed since the publication of this manual, write the ACA's Disabled Paddlers' Committee Clearinghouse. (Appendix 6) The Clearinghouse also has information on certified instruction and paddling opportunities.

**Please note:** The American Canoe Association and the authors do not endorse the following products or services. These adaptation suggestions have come from paddlers, instructors, organizations, and publications. Addresses of sources are listed in Appendix 6.

## Disability:
## Upper Limb-hand(s) impairment

*Problem:*
*Weakness in hand(s) and unable*
*to firmly grasp paddle.*

## Suggestions:

**Because swimming ability is affected, any adaptation that secures the hands to the paddle must be tried first with a wet exit under safe conditions.**

1. **Adapted Paddle Grip.** Build up the paddle shaft with waterproof tape, such as duct tape, or place a piece of foam pipe insulation where the paddler would grasp. Slit one side if necessary to fit the insulation over the shaft. Tape or use waterproof glue to hold it in place.

**Source:**     Hardware stores

2. **Bicycle Grips.** They can be cut, placed on the paddle, and secured with screws. The grips with finger groves help the paddler grasp.
**Source:**     Bicycle shops

3. **Velcro® Attachments.** Sew pile Velcro® on a glove and use waterproof glue or double-faced tape to attach loop Velcro® to the paddle shaft in the location where the hand would usually be placed while paddling. The Velcro® pieces attach when the hand grips the paddle, and they help to hold the hand in place.

## Suggestions:

Plastic Velcro® is available and when wet continues to have the same holding power. Use contact cement to attach plastic Velcro®.
**Source:**    Homemade.

4. **Adapted Hand Cuff.** Material such as waterproof nylon is formed, cut, or sewn into a rectangular shape to allow a paddler to slip her hand into it, up to the knuckles. Screw or staple the material into appropriate places on the paddle.
**Source:**    Homemade.

5. **Adapted Hand Grip.** An adapted hand grip can be made using disposable plastic cable ties that are opened and placed around the paddle shaft to hold a heavy piece of rubber such as a piece of used bicycle innertube in place. Mountain bike innertubes are ideal. The larger size of tie has a release tab which allows for adjustment, removal, and reuse. The hand is slid under the rubber up to the knuckles and should fit snugly under the tubing. The advantage to this adaptation is that it is not permanently attached making it ideal for use with rented equipment. Tightness and width can be adjusted. Trim excess tubing and ends of the cable ties.

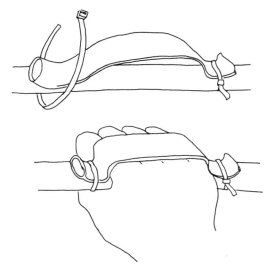

# Suggestions:

■ *Problem:*
*Weakness in hand(s) and unable*
*to firmly grasp paddle.*
*cont.*

**Source for cable ties:** Hardware stores, electronics stores, and auto parts stores. (This system can be used in conjunction with Hardbody's "Firm Fist Grips", see #6., below.)

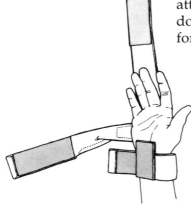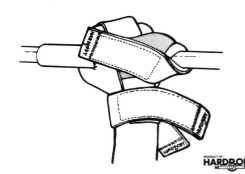

6. **Hardbody's "Firm Fist Grips".** This system of straps with Velcro® closures attaches the hand(s) to the paddle or a piece of exercise equipment. Using Velcro® cement, a piece of Velcro® is attached to the palm area of the "grip". The opposite piece of Velcro® is attached to the shaft of the paddle, either with double-faced tape for temporary use or glue for permanent placement.

The paddler puts the two straps around her hand and presses the palm Velcro® to the opposite Velcro® on the paddle. Then loop the final strap through the D-ring and attach the Velcro®. It is important that the tab over the hand can be reached easily for release by the teeth or opposite hand. Release of the paddle should be practiced repeatedly before using on the water. **Caution! This device prevents quick disengagement of the hand from the paddle and must be tried in a pool. Do not use this device on both hands at the same time because one hand needs to be more quickly released.** Adapted hand grip #5 or such can be used on the other hand.

## Suggestions:

**Source:** Hardbody Fitness Systems, Inc., approximately $40.00 a pair. (Appendix 6)

7. **Adapted Mitts.** Stitch ends of the fingertips of a glove together, or use a cotton or waterproof fabric mitt. Attach 1 piece of Velcro® to the middle of the mitt. A corresponding piece of Velcro® is sewn to Velcro® attached to the back of the middle of the mitt; when it is looped through the D-ring, the two pieces meet and hold.

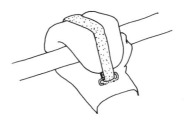

The paddler grabs the paddle. Loop the Velcro® through the D-ring and fasten snugly. You may want to wrap tape around the paddle just below the glove (where the person is grasping) to prevent the mitt from slipping. **Caution! This device prevents quick disengagement of the hand from the paddle and must be tried in a pool. Do not use this device on both hands at the same time because one hand needs to be more quickly released.** The adapted hand grip #5 or such can be used on the other hand.
    **Source:**    Homemade

■*Problem:*
*Shortened fingers unable to completely grasp the paddle.*

1. **Different Paddle.** First look for a small-diameter shaft on paddles. Look for oval grips as they are easier to hold onto than round ones. If necessary, adapt the shaft. Carve down areas of the wooden paddle where the paddler would grasp the paddle into an oval shape and sand well, but avoid destroying the strength of the paddle.
    **Source:**    Homemade.

## Disability:
## Upper Limb(s)/Amputation

■ *Problem:*
*Difficulty grasping paddle*

1. **Built-up Paddle Shaft.** Hold a single-bladed paddle under the stump. Build up the portion of the paddle held under the stump with closed-cell foam, or pipe insulation, etc. for easier grip and more comfort.

    **Source:**    Hardware stores and canoe/ kayak dealers

2. **Kickboard Paddle.** For a paddler with one arm, use a wooden kickboard of the type often used by swimmers, or similar sized, smooth lightweight wood (12 to 18 inches), with a handhold cut out. It is fatiguing to paddle with this adaptation.

    **Source:**    Homemade

3. **Adapted Paddle.** A paddle blade and part of the shaft is combined with a crutch-like upper portion.

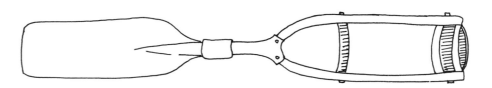

    **Source:**    Homemade

## Suggestions:

4. **Terminal Device.**TRS makes a terminal device (an attachment for a waterproof prosthesis) designed for holding onto a kayak or canoe paddle.

**Source:**   TRS, Inc. (Appendix 6)

## Disability:
## Neck and/or Trunk Impairment

■*Problem:
Limited neck
and/or rotation*

1. **Small Rear View Mirror.** Attach the mirror to glasses, sunglasses, or hat brim.
Source: Bicycle shops.

■*Problem:
Difficulty in
sitting stably*

1. Adaptations which provide seat support are described on page 54.

## Disability:
## Lower Limb(s) and/or Trunk Impairment

■*Problem:
Seated skin protection*

1. **Seat Padding.** Pad existing seat and back with closed-cell foam or neoprene. Use waterproof glue. The closed-cell will protect the paddler's skin from the abrasiveness of the existing fiberglass or plastic seat and will reduce the paddler's slipping in the seat.

(Ensolite® and mini-cell blue foam are closed-cell foams which will not absorb water and can be purchased at camping stores. Mini-cell

## Suggestions:

■*Problem:*
*Seated skin protection cont.*

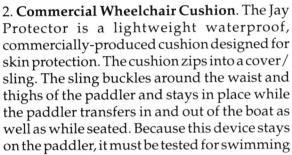

blue foam will not break down in ultraviolet light, but it is more expensive than Ensolite®.)

**Source:** Homemade

2. **Commercial Wheelchair Cushion.** The Jay Protector is a lightweight waterproof, commercially-produced cushion designed for skin protection. The cushion zips into a cover/sling. The sling buckles around the waist and thighs of the paddler and stays in place while the paddler transfers in and out of the boat as well as while seated. Because this device stays on the paddler, it must be tested for swimming ease.

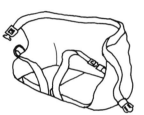

**Source:** Local wheelchair dealer, approximately $ 175.00.

3. **Clothing Padding.** Sew closed-cell foam padding into clothing or glue it inside the wet suit over bony prominences.

4. **Commercial Seats.** Wildwater Design's padded kayak seat is a foam seatbase which is placed on the existing kayak seat and could be attached to the existing boat seat. It is waterproof and provides contoured padding.

**Source:** Wildwater Design, approximately $35.00. (Appendix 6)

An individual who uses a wheelchair often uses a specialized cushion in her chair. The cushion is designed to provide support and to protect skin from breakdown. Many are not waterproof and must be kept dry. They cost approximately $350. Do not use them as the cushion for a canoe/kayak seat unless the individual requests that it be used.

## Suggestions:

▬▬▬▬▬▬▬▬▬▬▬▬▬▬▬▬

■ *Problem:*
*Difficulty entering kayak or canoe*

1. **Grab Handles**. Mounted on the boat, these handles help the paddler pull herself into the craft.

Mount them on the deck of a kayak or the gunwales of a canoe where they will be most helpful to the paddler. The paddler will need to try several locations before determining the best one for permanent placement. Foam blocks can be used if the finger grasp is not strong. **Caution**: be sure the placement of these handholds do not block a quick exit from the boat in the event of a capsize.

> **Source:** Any hardware store for commercially-made handles, or they can be made out of Ethafoam® or wood

2. **Backrests**. In sea kayaks with adjustable backrests, drop the backrest into the reclining position. **Caution**: Be sure that the deck behind the cockpit has been reinforced. (Cockpit Modifications, p. 54)

> **Source:** Adjustable backrests are standard features in some sea kayaks

■ *Problem:*
*Difficulty entering and exiting small cockpit on a kayak*

1. Buy a boat with a large cockpit opening or enlarge the cockpit opening. Lengthen and widen the front of the cockpit to the knees of the paddler. A new cockpit edge (combing) is formed and fiberglassed.
Source: Homemade.

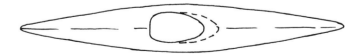

## Suggestions:

*■ Problem:*
*Difficulty in transferring*
*from a wheelchair down into a kayak*

1. **Mid-point Transfer**. Place an overturned milk crate or cooler between the wheelchair and the kayak or canoe. Pad the top with a towel. Transfer from the wheelchair to the mid-point, then to the kayak or the canoe. Reverse the transfer process when exiting the boat. By breaking the transfer into two parts, the total height of each transfer is more manageable.
    **Source:**    Homemade

2. **Cockpit Modifications**. Reinforce the kayak deck behind the cockpit. A support wall can be constructed using two to three inches of thick mini-cell foam cut precisely and glued with waterproof contact cement into the hull or held with stainless steel brackets. Glue a pad of closed-cell foam or neoprene to that deck. A pad can also be glued to the bottom of the kayak under the legs.

The paddler can transfer to the deck of the kayak behind the cockpit. The pad gives a non-slip area so the paddler can position her legs in the kayak and then ease herself into position in the kayak. The pad glued in the bottom of the kayak helps protect the skin.
    **Source:**    Canoe and kayak stores and hardware stores

3. **Sliding Pads**. Place an Ensolite® pad such as a sleeping bag pad on the back deck and into the boat. The paddler sits on the back deck and then slides down the boat. The Ensolite® pad slides with her into the kayak providing additional protection. Smooth wrinkles out of the pad.
    **Source:**    Camping goods stores

### Commercial Seats

*■ Problem:*
*Seat support*

1. **Removable Seat Backs** . The seat backs which offer some side support and the canoe seat can be covered with Ensolite® or a similar

## Suggestions:

closed-cell foam which will provide skin protection and help keep the paddler from sliding forward.

 A **Coleman Seat Back** is of a black vinyl grid design which hooks onto the canoe seat.

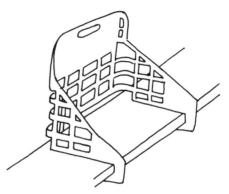

**Source:** Larger sporting goods stores, or order from Coleman, approximately$10.00.

 **Essex Industries' Portable Back Rest** is a canvas back with ash supports which help with side support.

**Source:** Essex Industries, approximately $20.00. (Appendix 6)

## Suggestions:

*■ Problem:
Seat support
cont.*

**Mad River Canoe Convertible Backrest** is a two position cane back rest which bolts to the canoe seat and stores under the seat when not in use. Does not have side support.

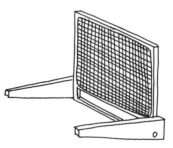

**Source:** Mad River Canoe Dealers, approximately $42.00. (Appendix 6)

2. **Sports/Beach Chairs** can be placed in the bottom of the canoe. They do give back support, but may not give lateral support. For stability, the chair must be secured to the canoe.

**Source:** Hardware stores, or sporting goods stores.

L.L. Bean Sports Chair, approximately $20.00. (Appendix 6)

## Suggestions:

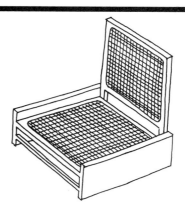

Mad River Canoe Folding Canoe Chair, approximately $70.00. (Appendix 6)

3. **Folding Lightweight Fabric Seat**. This seat with foam core provides back support but not side support. It does not attach to the canoe seat.

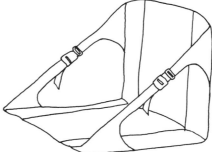

**Source:**   Crazy Creek Chair, from Crazy Creek Products or from many sporting goods stores, approximately $40.00. (Appendix 6)

# Suggestions:

*■ Problem:*
*Seat support*
*cont.*

4. **Partially-removable Back Supports.** Make them using aluminum or PVC poles and appropriate fabric. Cut the material for the seat backing wider than the distance between the poles used, to give a bowed effect and to keep the paddler's trunk in that pocket while giving extra lateral support.

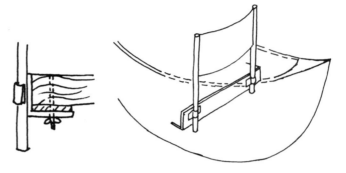

Source:    Hardware stores and fabric stores.

5. **Adjustable Seating System.** The American Canoe Association's adjustable adapted seating system is in development at the time of publishing. Contact the ACA Disabled Paddlers Committee.

## Custom-made Seats

6. **Seat Adaptations.** Use pieces of Ethafoam® and duct tape to adapt the seating area to give the paddler additional support. Pad Ethafoam® with nonabrasive material that does not absorb water. However, caution must be taken to assure that the paddler has a quick and clear exit. The placement of the foam pieces compensates for the lack of ability to brace against the kayak with the knees and feet.

Source:    Buy Ethafoam® from boating stores and duct tape from hardware stores.

## Suggestions:

**7. Ethafoam® Custom Seat.** Use a 2 to 3 foot piece of Ethafoam®. Cut and glue these pieces together as the diagram shows. After completing the initial cutting, use a sharp knife, sander or wood rasp to make appropriate indentations and contours. Then glue the seat together with waterproof glue, and cover it with Ensolite® or some other closed-cell foam. This seat must be securely attached to the boat to prevent sliding; waterproof glue can be used.

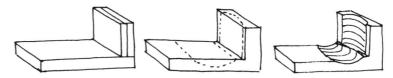

**Source:** Buy Ethafoam® and Ensolite® from canoe or kayak stores.

**8. Expanding Foam Seat.** Mix equal parts of X-40 Expanding Foam in a plastic trash bag. Place it in the kayak and sit on it. It expands forty times its original bulk. The paddler must be careful to hold herself up a bit, so the foam will also expand under her. The final product can be fiberglassed or used within a plastic covering. It will absorb water so it must be protected.

**Source:** Expanding Foam, Parts A and B, (both are needed) can be purchased from TAP Plastics. (Appendix 6)

**9. Molded Seat.** This seat construction is rather involved and requires some expertise working with fiberglass and some patience. A box three inches wider than the kayaker's hips and two feet long is filled with 5 to 6 inches of plaster of Paris. The plaster should look creamy, just about to set up, but still soft. A trash bag, or any thin plastic sheet, is then stretched over the plaster and the boater sits in the plaster to make a mold of her derriere.

## Suggestions:

■ *Problem:*
*Seat support*
*cont.*

This first cast should then be worked on to take out all wrinkles, bubbles, or imperfections so that a smooth surface is left. A bit of a hump between the thighs will help to keep the legs apart and give stability in the water. A gradual tip up at the front of the seat and under the thighs will aid in preventing the paddler from sliding forward.

After this first mold has been finished, it should be waxed with a good boat or car wax to prepare it for another casting. This cast will be off the original mold so that an exact replica, with modifications, of the boater's derriere will be made. This mold is then used as a form for the Ensolite®/fiberglass seat.

A piece of 1 inch Ensolite® is then fitted and glued to the bottom of this second mold or replica. Use rubber gloves for the glue, and try not to have too many seams in the Ensolite®. After custom fitting and glueing the foam onto the seat, all that is left is the fiberglassing process. Lay up fiberglass fabric on the bottom of the Ensolite® and when the resin has cured, peel off the plaster of Paris and clean off the residue.

A Yakima-type foot brace is then used to mount the seat on the floor of the kayak. The runner half of the brace is fiberglassed to the bottom of the kayak and the actual foot brace half is fitted to the front of the seat and fiberglassed on. This allows the seat to move back and forward to balance the boat and to be taken out, when needed. (Galland, 1980)

Other mediums can be used to make the first mold. Orthoplast® which is a sheet of moldable material often used by occupational therapists can be used or a cast can be made by an orthotist of the paddler's hips, buttocks, and thighs. Both of these require a specialist trained to work with these materials and so can be costly.

## Suggestions:

Note: Charlie Walbridge's <u>Boatbuilder's Manual</u> is an excellent source of information on working with fiberglass.

**Source:** Marine supply stores and hardware stores for the fiberglass. Ensolite® can be purchased at most camping stores. Yakima foot braces can be obtained through a kayak dealer or writing the company.

### Strap Systems

10. **Backstraps.** They provide back bracing and additional comfort and support. Attach them to the seat on the sides with bolts which need to be padded.

**Source:** Auto supply store for auto seat belt material.

11. **Seat Belt System.** Use of seat belts is controversial due to the danger of entrapment in the event of a capsize. Carefully assess the potential risks when using a seatbelt system. If another system can be designed that keeps the person in her seat and does not hinder the wet exit, try that system first before using seatbelts. (Seatbelts, p. 70)

If a seat belt is used, make it from a quick release airline seat belt or jet-ski buckle. Pad the belt over bony prominences in areas which lack sensation such as over hip bones. Devise one or two backup release systems e.g. a Velcro® closure on one side and another quick-release buckle on the other side in case the main seat belt buckle does not work. Also wearing a knife is recommended; if all systems fail, a knife can be used to cut the seatbelt.

■ *Problem:*
*Seat support*
*cont.*

**Caution: Seatbelts should only be used after extensive practice in a safe environment such as a pool or calm protected water with other people ready to assist.**

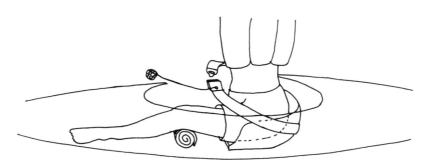

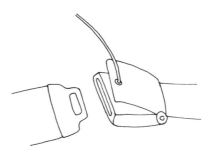

Attach the seatbelt to the seat itself or low on the inside of the hull. If mounted too high on the sides, the strap offers little support to a student trying to stay in the boat to complete an Eskimo roll. Attach to the release buckle a length of parachute cord with a whiffle ball or large knot (monkey paw) at its end. This cord runs outside the skirt and hangs at the front or side of the cockpit, depending on the student's preference. When the paddler pulls the toggle, the skirt releases as well as the lap belt.

**Source:**     Auto parts stores for the seat belt material.

## Disability:
## Lower Limb(s) Impairment

**■ Problem:**
*Balance*

Paddlers with amputations and/or who are para/quadriplegics with significant loss of muscle mass in the lower limb(s) may have difficulty maintaining balance of the boat.

1. **Seat Adaptations.** Drop the seat two to four inches to lower the paddler's center of gravity.
    **Source:** Homemade. Check with canoe/kayak dealer for the best method to do this.

2. **Ballast.** Compensate for the weight loss with **ballast.** Use non-breakable wide-mouth containers filled with sand, water, peanut butter *(then you're ready for lunch)*, etc. Duct tape the containers to the center line of the kayak to balance the kayak. Put the ballast in balanced pairs to compensate for general weight loss or on the side of the amputation to compensate for weight loss on that side.
    **Source:** Sporting good stores or empty food containers.

**■ Problems:**
*Leg spasms or discomfort from over-extension when seated in a kayak or on the bottom of a canoe; knee hyperextension, and/or paddler tends to slide forward in the seat.*

1. **Knee Padding.** Place a roll of non-water absorbing foam 4 to 6 inches in diameter under the knees. By keeping the knees flexed, the muscles tend to stay more relaxed. The roll under the knees also helps to keep the paddler from sliding forward in the seat.

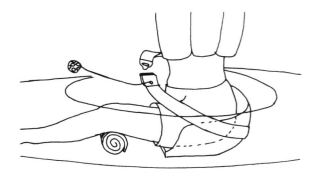

**Caution: Be sure the roll will not block easy exit from the kayak if a wet exit is necessary.** Practice wet exits with the roll in place and with assistance ready nearby. This adaptation is also helpful when sitting on the bottom of a canoe.

      **Source:**    Camping goods stores.

■ *Problem:*
*Feet slide out of place on the canoe bottom causing the paddler to slide in the seat*

1. **Non-slip Material.** Place a piece of material, e.g. SlipStop® with non-slip surfaces on both sides, on the canoe bottom under the paddler's feet. Place the paddler's feet on the material in a comfortable position. Because the feet rest on the non-slip material and are not attached to it, the paddler's feet simply fall away from the material in the event of a capsize.

      **Source:**    Cleo, Inc. (Appendix 6) Other brands are available such as Dicem®, etc. and are often used by occupational therapists.

■ *Problem:*
*Getting the boat to the water*

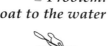

1. **Sliding.** Buy a durable boat that will endure sliding over the ground, e.g. ABS, rotomolded plastic, etc.

2. **Waxing.** Wax the bottom of the boat for easier sliding.

3. **Protective Coverings.** An additional layer of material similar to that of the boat can be attached to the bottom to protect the craft when sliding it along the ground. Such protective coverings are available in kit form, e.g. grunch plate.

      **Source:**    Canoe and kayak dealers

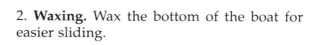

4. **Ground Cover.** Obtain a piece of scrap carpet or piece of canvas and place this material on the ground at the place where you launch. The boat is placed on this material. It helps prevent damage to the bottom of the canoe/kayak and provides a good surface for

sliding the boat into and out of the water. It can be folded and easily stored.

5. **Boat cart.** Purchase a boat cart designed for transporting a boat easily across the ground.

**Source:**   Canoe and kayak stores.

6. **Reverse Entry**. Try backing down to the water in the kayak. Pushing backwards is often easier than pushing forwards.

7. **Ski Poles**. Cut off two ski poles below the grips at a length which allows a paddler sitting in the kayak to reach the ground. The kayaker grips the poles and propels herself towards the water over the land. The poles provide better traction against the ground than a paddler's hands.
**Source:**   Ski shop.

# Disability: Hearing Impairment

■ *Problem: Unable to hear without a hearing aid*

1. **Water-resistant Hearing Aid**. After much experimentation with other models, a kayak instructor (Poudre River Kayak, Fort Collins, CO) recommends the HB-35 hearing aid made by Rion which she uses. Cover the ear hole in the paddling helmet to reduce the amount of water reaching the aid.
**Source:**   Rion Acoustic Instruments, Inc. (Appendix 6).

## Disability:
## Visual Impairment

*■ Problem:
Visual (determining
the position of
the blade of
the paddle*

1. **Blade Angle Indicator**. Use tape on the paddle shaft in line with the blade edge. Wrap waterproof tape (bicycle, duct, etc. ) around a popsicle stick, tongue depressor, foam strip, or matchstick to provide a better "index". Place the tape on the paddle shaft near the paddler's thumb where she can easily feel it in order to check the position of the paddle blade.

**Source:**     Homemade

*■ Problem:
Unable to read compass
when navigating.*

1. " Silva Directional Compass" with a Braille face.

**Source:**     American Foundation for the Blind. (Appendix 6)

*Unneccessary adaptations!*

# CHAPTER SEVEN

# *Rescues*

A primary concern is the safety of the participants. Knowledge and skill help to minimize dangers, but they cannot be completely eliminated in an adventure sport such as canoeing and kayaking. As stated in the ACA Canoeing and Kayaking Instruction Manual , "Every paddler must be prepared to accept the consequences of an error in skill or judgement that leads to a swamped craft. Tipping over and swimming rapids are an integral part of canoesport. Paddlers must be prepared to accept the responsibility of rescuing themselves and, if possible, the rescuing of others.

A goal of paddling instruction is the education and training of participants in rescue techniques. Students should understand that each rescue situation is unique and usually requires one or more rescue techniques appropriate to a given situation. The development of the proper skills is a necessary part of a student's experience, and knowing a variety of rescue techniques is valuable."

### *Never paddle alone-your life may depend on aid from another paddler.*

Rescue practice is essential. Early in her instruction every student able and disabled should wet exit and practice a rescue technique appropriate to the type of boat she will be paddling. All rescues must be practiced in a safe place e.g. pool or shallow protected area, where the instructor can stand. Practice the rescues before they might be needed.

---

**It is not a good time to try them when the wind is blowing, it's hailing, the water temperature is 48°, or two Great White Sharks are circling your yum yum yellow boat and you have heard they like yellow.**

---

This preliminary capsize and rescue practice allows the student to experience the aspect of paddling that she most dreads and to sense control in being able to manage her rescue in a safe environment.

We cannot overemphasize the importance of practicing wet exits (tipping over) and rescues in a safe, controlled environment before they are needed. You cannot expect that you will be able to stand on the bottom to get back in the boat or to help someone get back into her boat in most open-water situations. More rescue boats may be needed for a class which includes paddlers with disabilities to help with re-entry, or to stabilize the boat. The instructor can make that determination during rescue practice.

Rescues must be completed quickly to prevent immersion hypothermia. In water, a paddler loses heat 32 times faster than in the air.

The order of rescue priorities is always the person first, then the boat, and then the equipment. Because this manual deals with the specifics of instruction of persons with disabilities, this section does not include a general discussion of kayak and canoe rescues.

Issues such as designation of the primary rescue boat, the backup boat, who aids the capsized paddler, assessment, stand-by assistance, avoidance of conversion, etc., must be planned before any outing. It is important to consult a general guide to canoeing/kayaking for details on general rescue techniques and ideally to take a rescue class. The ACA Canoeing and Kayaking Instruction Manual and Fundamentals of Coastal Kayaking Manual for Instructors, and Les Bechdel's River Rescue are excellent sources of information on rescues. Included here are rescues which have been found to be effective with paddlers with disabilities. Every instructor should practice rescues with the paddler in a safe, controlled environment instead of assuming that the rescues she generally uses will be sufficient for a person with a disability. Preplanning is vital.

## SELF-RESCUES

Waiting for someone to rescue you is never as good as self-rescue. In cold water, the paddler's strength goes quickly, so speed in a rescue is extremely important.

**Waiting for a rescue upside down while your head is bouncing around over rocks is not the best way to see rivers.**

The best self-rescue method for all paddlers in a kayak is the Eskimo roll because the paddler does not exit her boat and is submerged in the water for only seconds.

*Eskimo Rolling*
The following section on Eskimo rolling includes techniques which have been used to teach rolling to people with lower limb impairments. It is not a general guide to Eskimo rolling. For a comprehensive book on rolling use Derek Hutchinson's Eskimo Rolling. Clear drawings and descriptions fill this excellent guide to teaching and learning Eskimo rolls.

The ability to roll gives the paddler confidence to enjoy more challenging bodies of water. Rolling is a skill which requires practice. It is more difficult without the use of hips or legs, but it is not impossible. Granted, rolling is easier to do using good hip motion, but this is not necessary.

All kayak paddlers should try to learn an Eskimo roll. Without one, the paddler will have to rely on other less effective self-rescue techniques or on other paddlers for rescue.

A positive attitude on the part of the instructor and the student is the first step. The choice of kayak design is also important. Choose a comfortable, stable boat with a flat bottom and rounded sides.

Use an easy-to-roll kayak for learning in the pool and then practice with the boat that the paddler usually uses. Learning to roll in an easier boat at first will reduce the frustration that occurs in trying to roll. The mastered techniques can then be transferred to the paddler's usual boat.

More important than hull shape, however, is the outfitting that keeps the paddler in place in the seat. When the boat is halfway up, the paddler who is not firm in her seat will slide to the side or front which may prevent completion of the roll.

A tight neoprene skirt, as well as a small-volume boat with padded knee and thigh braces, will help hold the person in place for pool practice. However, problems arise when the person wants to wet exit. Because she is so tight in the boat she may be unable to get free. Tight, secure systems with small cockpits, thigh braces, and knee braces should be tried repeatedly in a safe environment such as a pool. At least three people should be with the paddler to right the boat in case of difficulty with exiting. Wet exits should always be practiced after any new

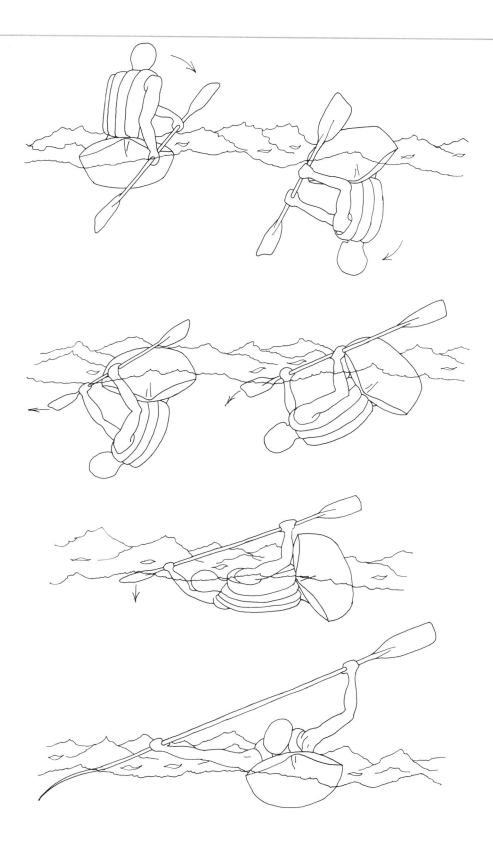

*Eskimo Rolls*

adaptations are made. The paddler must practice using adapted seating systems and bracing systems, until wet exits are quick and reliable.

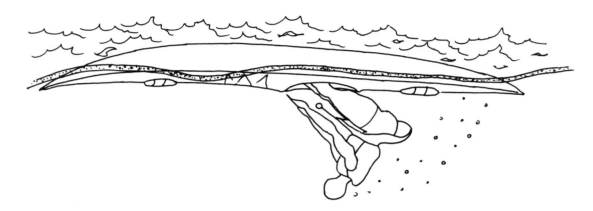

Use of seat belts is very controversial because they can be dangerous. Extreme caution and preparation should be taken if they are used. The paddler must practice wet exits and seat belt releases in a safe, supervised environment. Only when the release is an easy, automatic response and the wet exit is quick, should the use of a seat belt be considered for general paddling situations.

In case the release buckle fails, have at least one reliable backup system such as attaching the belt to the boat with quick-release Velcro®. The belt should be made of wide style straps that pull over the student's lap and fasten with a large quick-release airline or jet ski buckle. (Seat belts, p. 61)

For a person with limited control of her legs, put padding in the kayak between the legs so they do not fall to the low side of the boat when the kayak turns on its side. Duct tape a long tube, padded with closed-cell foam, on the bottom of the boat which will keep the legs on either side of the kayak during Eskimo rolls or while doing braces. Make sure that the padding does not restrict the paddler exiting the boat when it capsizes.

In the pool, three instructors or helpers per craft are recommended when teaching rolling to increase the margin of safety. One person can stand next to the student and the other two can be positioned at the ends of the kayak on the opposite side of the boat from the first instructor. Using at least three people is recommended in order to share the weight when lifting or righting the kayak in the pool and to decrease the risk of back injury to the instructors.

Caution must also be taken when helping a capsized paddler back into the boat to avoid unnecessary injury to her skin. Care must be taken to avoid injuring the student's shoulder(s) when righting the kayak with the shoulder lift.

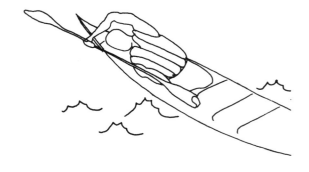

*Other Suggestions:*

- Derek Hutchinson mentions the use of thigh boards in <u>Eskimo Rolling</u> to keep a person in the kayak. **Thigh boards** are pieces of wood placed across the paddler's thighs and under the cockpit rim. Thigh boards are used only in an instructional session, in a safe environment like a pool, and with several instructors or safety people with the student.

- Try using a long paddle and an extended paddle grip (hands offset to one end of the paddle. The extended grip allows the paddler to extend the length of the useable paddle area which gives the stroke the advantage of more leverage. A survival roll is an Eskimo roll which uses an extended paddle grip.

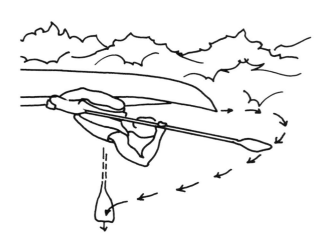

- A paddle float may also add buoyancy to the end of the working blade.

- Check inside the boat for sharp edges and remove the foot pegs if the paddler has limited use of her legs.

- Foot protection should be worn in the kayak, e.g. wet suit booties, sneakers, etc.

- A Steyr or back deck roll (see p. 69) is the easiest to learn because the body is kept close to the deck and reduces the force necessary to right the boat. However, caution must be used in shallow water due to the risk of injury to the face. Using a back deck roll or even a survival roll is preferable to a long swim as lengthy exposure to the cold water is always a concern. In the ocean or deep lakes, scraping your face on the bottom is not a problem. After learning the back deck roll, it is easier to learn a front deck roll. The front deck roll is better for rocky, shallow rivers as the face is protected while doing the roll. After a person with reduced or no use of her stomach muscles rolls with a back deck roll, she may need to pull herself into a sitting position by pulling on the cockpit with her hand. She will need to hold the paddle in one hand and pull herself up with the other.

- Be aware that, with some disabilities, spasms may occur when the person leans all the way back on the deck. The instruction will have to wait until the spasms cease.

- Try 180° rolls to start and then go to 360°'s.

### Paddle Float Rescue

The paddle float rescue method is excellent for ocean boating, but is not recommended for whitewater rivers. It is a good self-rescue method for a person with poor balance because the body is kept low to the kayak in re-entry. (p. 73)
Directions:
1. Right the kayak.
2. Position yourself on the downwind side of the kayak and hold onto the kayak and paddle.

3. Place paddle float on the paddle and inflate.
4. Secure paddle to the rear deck at right angles to the center line of the kayak in order to prevent it from pivoting when you use it.
5. Swim and hoist your body up on the stern deck. You should be laying chest down on the deck.
6. Place one foot into the boat, then the other.
7. Keeping your weight on the float, pivot into the seat.
8. Put on your sprayskirt and pump out the boat.

### GROUP RESCUES

When rescuing, one must be cautious not to injure the paddler being rescued. For example, care must be taken to avoid shoulder injury when assisting re-entry into a canoe/kayak. The paddler could be pulled by her PFD or waistband. Skin can be injured when dragging a person into a boat. If possible, pad the gunwale or cockpit lip before pulling the paddler into the boat. Rescues must be done quickly, but not in such a hurry as to injure someone.

### Eskimo Rescue (giving a nose)

This method only works when paddling partners have practiced it, have confidence in their ability to work together and have an understanding of when its use is appropriate. Timing is important and the rescuer must be close at hand.

The capsized paddler remains upside-down in her boat and holds onto her paddle if possible, while banging on the bottom of her kayak. This action signals her partner that she needs assistance, and the partner can

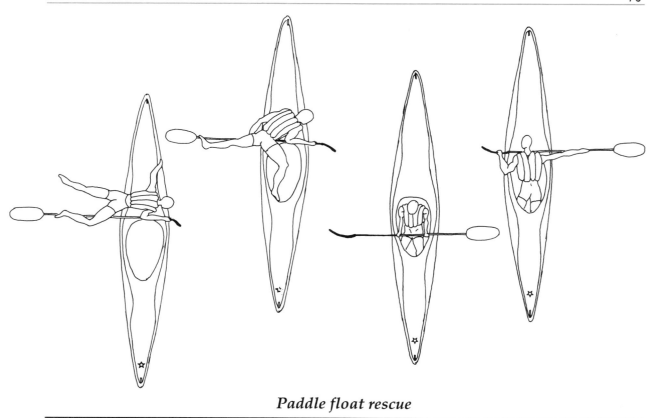

*Paddle float rescue*

*Eskimo rescue - "Giving a nose"*

paddle her kayak over to the overturned kayak and try to put the bow/nose of her boat as near as possible to the upside-down person's hands. The submerged paddler should be moving her hands back and forth beside the boat to locate the rescue boat easier. She can then hold onto the nose of the rescue boat and right her boat by using hip motion or muscle.

**One of Annie's friends turned over on a large volume river and was contemplating how to get organized for her roll, when suddenly she heard loud pounding on the bottom of her boat. She figured she had died and her Maker was knocking. To her relief it was one of her paddling partners who had quickly moved into the Eskimo rescue position.**

### "Cling and Jerk" Rescue

In rapids, it is often difficult to get one's bow precisely into the imploring hands of the upside-down boater. Instead of using the Eskimo rescue, the rescuer paddles up to an overturned paddler's boat and pulls up parallel to it. From this position, the rescuer can reach **over** the paddler's boat, grab the cockpit rim, and pull the boat halfway up. It helps if the paddler leans forward or backward to assist in righting the boat. The rescuer then pulls on the neck of the paddler's PFD to complete the righting. This method does not take exceptional strength, and it is very stable because the two boats form an effective catamaran.

### The Scoop Method

The scoop rescue method is an easy technique to help a capsized paddler who is weak in the upper body, has limited use of her legs, or is very tired. This method is best on the ocean or lakes. On rivers obstacles such as rocks, strainers, and holes make this rescue method unsafe. It also requires more time than would be practical on a fast moving river.

The rescuer first takes the capsized person's paddle and secures it during the rescue. Next the rescuer paddles beside the capsized craft and turns the boat on its side with the cockpit facing away from the rescue boat. The capsized paddler should be next to the overturned kayak, not between the two kayaks. While on her back, the paddler can guide her floating legs inside the cockpit of the overturned craft and float her body towards the front of the kayak. If she is unable to do so, assistance for this step of the method will be needed. When her buttocks are even with the seat of the kayak, she holds onto the upper edge of the kayak with the hand that will be on that side of the kayak when it is righted. She then tells the rescuer that she is ready and the rescuer pulls down on the high side of the kayak and rights it. The paddler will be in the boat. The rescuer supports the craft until the paddler is settled and balanced. The kayak is then pumped, skirt refastened and the paddle returned.

*Scoop rescue*

If another rescuer is present, she can move next to the capsized paddler and help lift under the shoulders of the paddler at the same time the other rescuer is righting the kayak.

This scoop rescue method also works well while practicing wet exits and rolls in a pool. Instead of getting the person out of the pool and then back into the boat, this method saves time and is easier on paddlers who have limited use of their lower limbs and/or tire easily.

In the pool, one instructor stands next to the student and can help guide her floating legs into the kayak, if necessary. Once the student is next to the kayak and her buttocks are even with the back of the seat, the instructor lifts the student's shoulders while the other instructors rotate the kayak into the upright position.

## Boat Over Boat Rescues

If the capsize has resulted in the paddler getting out of the boat, she should remain with her kayak/canoe, holding onto the upstream end and her paddle. The rescuer should approach the capsized kayak/canoe and grab one end of it. Now the paddler can give her paddle to the rescuer. The paddler holds onto one end of the rescuer's boat as the rescuer pulls the upside-down kayak up onto her deck. By rocking the upside down boat from end to end, the water is emptied out. The kayak/canoe is then turned upright and placed next to the other boat as a catamaran. The rescuer helps the paddler get back into her boat by supporting her boat and lifting her PFD or waistband.

*Boat over boat rescue*

### Towing a Paddler in Her Boat

A weak or tired student can be towed in her boat for a while in order to rest. In a windy lake, for example, there might be a section that the group is going to cross that involves strong head winds. A weak paddler could be towed across the difficult section to a calmer stretch where she could then resume paddling. Be sure to discuss towing with the person first as it can be embarrassing to be towed.

The towing system should be of the quick release type in order for the towed boat to be released easily if a safety problem arises. It is better to run the towing line through the stern line of the towing boat in order to help keep the following boat in a straight line. The paddler who is resting can simply rest her paddle on the front deck of her kayak during the towing or store it in her canoe.

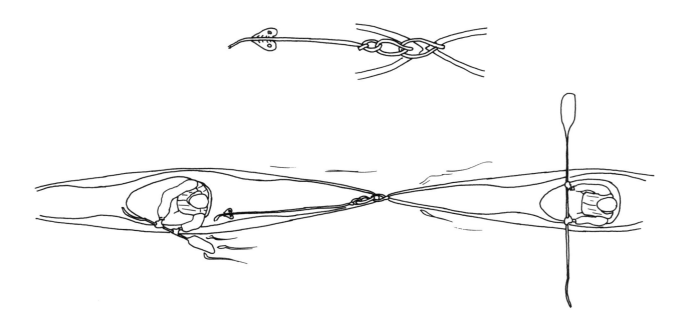

# CHAPTER EIGHT

# A Primer on Paddling Trips

Paddling trips with people who are able and disabled work well. The group shares a common goal of experiencing both paddling and nature. This is a time apart from the usual routine of life. On both day and multi-day trips, individuals must meet the challenges of the environment. Teamwork is essential on all trips and each person's talents can add to the group. Individual respect is rightfully earned.

Advanced planning alleviates potential obstacles. All participants must understand that the group will consist of participants who are able and disabled. The leaders need to understand what assistance will be needed by those with disabilities and preplan for that assistance. A thorough paddler's interview is necessary. Always bear in mind the guidelines for disclosure of medical information. Consider the following suggestions when planning able/disabled trips:

**Ratio Of Skilled Paddlers To Paddlers With Disabilities.** Assuming the paddlers with disabilities are not skilled paddlers, the ratio on a trip is determined by a number of important factors: the length and difficulty of the trip, the skill level and experience of all paddlers, and the type and severity of the disabilities involved. Making a decision about the ratio comes from experience, but it is always better to have a few more experienced people along than you think you need. For example, six people who are able-bodied to one person with a disability is not necessary

and may actually limit the participation of the paddler with the disability by overprotecting that paddler.

**Route Selection.** Scout the route of a trip prior to departure with the group. It is essential that each individual have access to the campsites. Make sure that all individuals are able to move around on the site, including access to the water and latrine.

**Repair Kit.** Carry additional Ensolite® and more duct tape if seating adaptations have been made. On a trip with people who have wheelchairs, take a tire pump, patching kit, and tools such as an allen wrench. This is the responsibility of the owner of the wheelchair, but the instructor should make sure these items are packed.

**Portages.** Many people in wheelchairs can travel over the more level, well-cleared portages. Uneven rocky terrain and overgrown bush are far more difficult. If there is any doubt about a paddler's ability to manage a portage, the instructor may want to make an assessment with the paddler on similar terrain prior to the trip.

**Wheelchairs and Walking Aids.** It is necessary to take wheelchairs and walking aids on trips so that the person has mobility on land. Many wheelchairs can be folded and placed on the bottom in the center of a canoe. Secure the wheelchair to the canoe (usually to one of the thwarts) to prevent it from shifting during paddling and so it is not lost in the event of a capsize. Practice rescues with the wheelchair tied in the canoe. Battery-powered wheelchairs are too heavy to be lifted and are not appropriate for wilderness settings.

**Medications.** Medications must be carried in waterproof containers. The paddler should check with her pharmacist or doctor for proper storage. If emergency medicine like a bee sting kit is needed, it should be carried in the paddler's boat. A duplicate set of required medicines should also be carried in another boat.

**Guide Dogs.** A person who uses a guide dog will want to take her dog on the trip to give her mobility when on land.

**Levels of Independence.** One must decide the minimum level of independence for day-to-day activities (such as dressing, basic self care, and ability to care for bowel and bladder function) on an extended trip. If a personal care attendant (PCA) is needed for daily routine, the person who needs this care should bring the caretaker along. The attendant **must** participate in pretrip instruction and safety classes.

One cannot expect most wilderness areas to be accessible to wheelchairs, and there are many situations when it is not practical to bring one. A person with a mobility impairment may have to accept being carried to and from her boat to the campsite and to the latrine. A person with upper body strength can bring cushions, for example, a Jay Protector, boat cushion, etc., along to make it easier to scoot around on the ground. To lessen the feeling of dependence, a person with a disability can handle other trip chores such as planning the logistics, planning the menus, shopping for food and supplies, setting up tents, cooking meals, washing dishes, and packing common gear when breaking camp.

**Personal Hygiene.** Important considerations include the following:
- Provide non-embarrassing opportunities to go to the bathroom/latrine. A windscreen can be put in front of the latrine if the latrine is not located in a private place.
- The latrine needs to be accessible.
- If wheelchairs are used on the trip, the latrine needs to be wheelchair accessible.

Unfortunately, many people who would like to go on long day trips or multi-day trips are stymied about how to deal with bowel and bladder routines. Here are some ideas that have been successfully tried by spinal cord injured paddlers, male and female:

**Catheter/Leg Bags.** When paddling long distances, catheter/leg bags may be emptied into wide-mouth quart-size poly bottles and dumped in a proper location.

**Urination.** When paddling on salt water, it is acceptable to urinate right into the water.

**Catheterization in a Wheelchair.** A woman who does intermittent catheterization and takes her wheelchair along can learn to catheterize herself in her chair.

**Catheterization in a Folding Chair.** Use a very lightweight aluminum folding chair with a cloth seat and backrest. It sits about four inches above the ground and can be carried very easily on the back deck of a sea kayak or can be lashed in a canoe. The advantage of the folding chair is its portability and it allows the individual to urinate without exposing the skin to the ground. There is also less chance that the paddler will wet herself. An added advantage is that the folding chair is also very comfortable to use as a camp chair.

**Portapotty.** If a portapotty is used by the group, set it up in a very stable position with, if possible, a side or back rest; a tree or a rock can work well. At the very least, provide a person with poor sitting balance with something to grab. Use a portapotty with long legs for paddlers in wheelchairs, when there is sufficient storage space to transport this equipment.

**Portapotty Alternatives.** Sea kayakers or river boaters who cannot take a large portapotty have other options for managing bowel movements. A raised toilet seat is easy to assemble and dismantle for packing into small places. Place it over a previously-dug hole, then transfer onto it. This stable seat keeps the person off the ground.

**Waste Removal.** Another method, especially when it is necessary to carry all human wastes out of the area, is laying in your tent on your side on a large piece of heavyweight aluminum foil to defecate. Wrap up the entire package and place in a Zip Lock® bag for later disposal.

### Interviewing A Potential Outfitter

As an instructor or group leader, you may need to select an outfitter for an outing. A group which includes individuals with physical disabilities should ask the following basic questions before choosing an outfitter for a day or multi-day trip:
- What is the outfitter's experience with paddlers with physical disabilities?
- What is their safety record?
- What training do the leaders have in first aid and CPR?
- What adaptive equipment do they have?
- Do they have references from paddlers with disabilities?
  Ask these follow-up questions to help assess the mindset of the outfitter:
- Do you feel every person who has a physical disability should be accompanied by a person who is able-bodied?

- How do you determine the level of assistance that a person may need?

Their responses will help you to decide if they view people who have disabilities as individuals with a wide range of abilities or as dependent, regardless of the disability. There is no one right or wrong answer. But attitude can make or break a trip, so find a way to get a feeling for the outfitter's attitudes.

It is important that the group leader and the outfitter be willing to accept input from each other. Be sure responsibilities, etc., are clearly defined in advance.

### Types of Carries

Being carried can be an humiliating experience. When it appears necessary to carry a person, involve her in the discussion from the beginning. First, review all alternatives to carrying. If no other solution is found, ask the person if she is willing to be carried.

The safety and dignity of a carry comes from preplanning. Discuss all details of the carry before beginning. Determine how the person will be picked up, and how to protect the person being lifted as well as the lifter. When lifting, always bend at the knees and keep the lower back straight, using leg strength, rather than back strength.

Be sure spotters are prepared in case the lifter loses her balance.

**Orthodox:** Best when lifters are approximately the same height. Each lifter places an arm around the lower back of the person to be carried. The lifters place their other arm under the middle of the thighs. The arms under the legs can be linked by a double forearm grasp or double wrist grasp.

See illustrations next page.

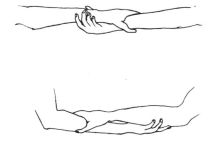

is kept secure without putting strain on her shoulders. The second lifter can either lift from the side or from astride the legs of the person being carried depending on the setting. With this carry there is uneven distribution of weight between the lifters. The taller lifter at the head will carry most of the weight. This lift is not recommended for uneven ground or long distances. It is best for lifting off the floor or when transferring sideways.

*Orthodox*

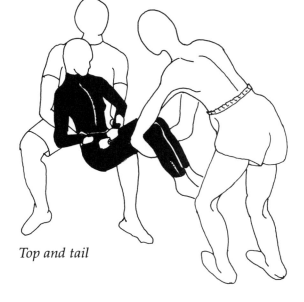

*Top and tail*

**Top and Tail:** Best when lifters are of different heights. The person to be carried crosses her arms across her chest and grasps her own wrists. The taller lifter stands behind the person to be carried and places her arms under those of the person to be carried and grasps the forearms of the person to be carried. It is more comfortable for the person to be carried if the lifters' thumbs are placed on top of the forearms to avoid pinching the skin. The lifter at the head leads the lift and by squeezing her forearms to the sides of the person being carried, the person being carried

**Piggy-Back:** The person being carried must have strong shoulders. The lifter stoops in front of the person to be carried. The person to be carried grasps around the shoulders of the lifter. The spotter can assist in moving the legs of the person to be carried around the lifter. Use a spotter behind the person being carried. The spotter can place her hands under the buttocks of the person being carried (with her permission) and lift slightly, reducing the strain on the arms of the person being carried and also lightening the load on the lifter. Be sure not to push the carrier off balance. If the person to be carried can do so, she could reach over the shoulders of the carrier, and grasp her own ankles, thus freeing the hands of the carrier. This is easier for people with long strong arms. This carry is useful for narrow passages and over difficult terrain.

## ON-WATER COMMUNICATION

Signals, whistles, etc. necessary for all paddlers.

Communication on the water is necessary when there is an emergency or when routine information needs to be shared with other paddlers in the group. Prior to departure, review the signals clearly with everyone in the group.

The following general guidelines apply:
- Do not depend on voice commands.
- Simple is best in signals. The purpose is to attract attention.
- Hand and paddle signals can be used on rivers.
- Plan a backup system to use if the first signal does not attract attention.
- Every paddler should have a U. S. Coast Guard approved waterproof signal whistle attached to her PFD.

- Whistles are **only** to be used for **emergencies**.

On the river, the American Whitewater Affiliation Universal River Signals (p. 82) are useful. However, they do not work if the other paddlers are not looking or when paddling on large bodies of water. If the group includes a paddler who is hearing impaired or visually impaired, adapt the signals to be used. For example, use a bright orange flag signal for a paddler who is hearing impaired or a clanging device for a paddler who is visually impaired.

Open-water paddling (lakes and oceans) requires additional signaling techniques. Sound may not carry as well depending on water and weather conditions. Cannister air horns are good backup signaling systems.

With greater distances, visibility may be difficult. Bright-colored PFDs, helmets, boat decks, paddle blades, and/or use of reflecting tape increase the visibility. Hand-held flares are effective. The Fundamentals of Coastal Kayaking Manual for Instructors (ACA) contains extensive information on signaling devices for open-water paddling.

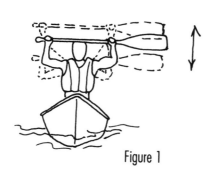

Figure 1

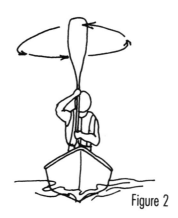

Figure 2

*STOP: Potential hazard ahead. Wait for "all clear" signal before proceeding, or scout ahead.* Form a horizontal bar with your paddle or outstretched arms. Move this bar up and down to attractr attention, using a pumping motion with the paddle or a flying motion with your arms. Those seeing the signal should pass it back to others in the party. (Figure 1)

*HELP/EMERGENCY: Assist the signaler as soon as possible.* Give three long blasts on a police whistle while waving a paddle, helmet or PFD over your head in a circular motion. If you do not have a whistle, use the visual signal alone. A whistle is best carried on a lanyard attached to the shoulder of a PFD. (Figure 2)

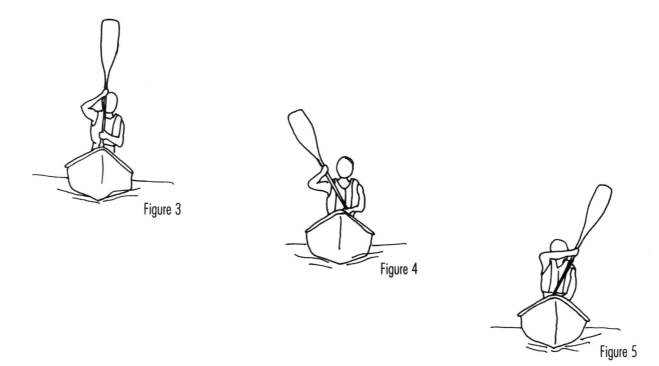

Figure 3

Figure 4

Figure 5

*ALL CLEAR: Come ahead. (in the absence of other directions, proceed down the center.)* Form a vertical bar with your paddle or with one arm held high above your head. Turn the paddle blade flat for maximum visibility. To signal direction or a preferred course through a rapid or around an obstruction, lower the previous vertical "all clear" signal by 45 degrees toward the side of the river with the preferred route. Never point toward the obstacle you wish to avoid. (Figures 3-4-5)

# *Conclusion*

That's it! You now have the tools to get started. Follow the guidelines. Use the information that fits the paddler's needs.  Above all, work *with* the paddler. Together you can do it. The joy of paddling is waiting and you are the key!

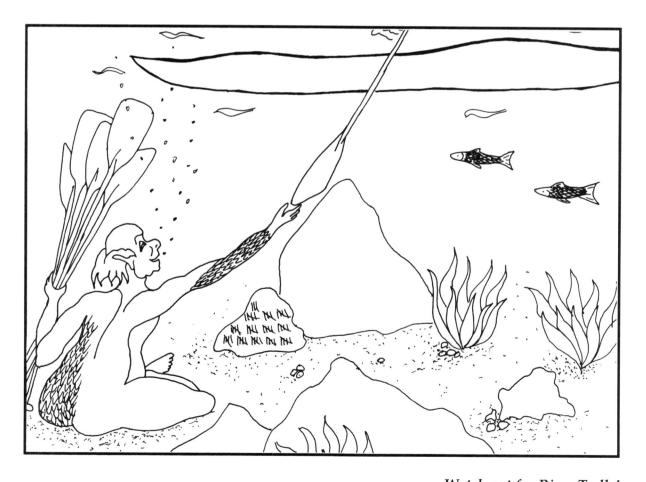

*Watch out for River Trolls!*

# GLOSSARY

Difficulties may arise when an instructor is unfamiliar with the effects of a specific disability and how that disability may affect the student's paddling. Although it is important to have a basic understanding of potential limitations, one need not be a medical authority on every disease or condition before instructing people with physical disabilities. A brief glossary has been included in an attempt to clarify more common terms and conditions. The list is by no means exhaustive and you may wish to investigate further to learn more about a specific disability. Some cautions and additional information are added which are not part of the definitions of the terms. Remember, it is essential to look at each individual's **abilities** relative to paddling, regardless of the diagnosis or condition.

## AMPUTEE
A person who has lost one or more limbs. The type of amputation is usually classified according to location, e.g. right below the knee amputation.

## ARTHRITIS
An inflammatory condition involving the joints.

## BILATERAL
Both sides of the body; frequently used to describe amputations to both sides of the body, e.g. bilateral below the knee amputations.

## CATHETER
A slender hollow tube inserted into a body passage, e.g. into the bladder to draw off urine, connected to a collection container "leg bag" or used intermittently.

## CEREBRAL PALSY
A non-progressive condition occurring in the early stages of life (up to approximately 2 years of age), resulting in damage to certain parts of the brain with subsequent loss or impairment of muscle control and possibly sensation. There is a great deal of variation in the degree of involvement.

## COLOSTOMY
Surgical creation of an opening for feces to pass through the abdominal wall.

## DECUBITUS ULCERS
Pressure sores which are caused by sitting too long without proper padding, poor circulation, etc.

## DIABETES MELLITUS
A disease involving insulin deficiency, and characterized by an excess of sugar in the blood and urine. Diabetes can be controlled with diet and medication in most cases.

## EPILEPSY
Seizure disorder.

## FATIGUE
Loss of strength or exhaustion. This is a frequent problem with many disabilities.

## FLACCID
Lack of muscle tone.

## HEARING IMPAIRMENT
Partial or complete loss of hearing.

## HEMIPLEGIA

Some degree of impairment of muscles and/or sensation in the arm and leg on one side of the body; may have flaccid or spastic muscles.

## LOWER EXTREMITIES

Refers to legs.

## LUNG DISEASE

A chronic disorder involving the lungs or mechanics of breathing, e.g. asthma, emphysema, and neurological or muscle disorders impairing the respiratory muscles. **Asthma** is a chronic disease characterized by labored breathing or wheezing.

## MULTIPLE SCLEROSIS

A relapsing disease of the central nervous system affecting various parts of the body; may produce fatigue, weakness, poor balance, tremor, decreased sensation, and muscle paralysis.

## MUSCLE SPASMS

A sudden involuntary contraction of a muscle or a group of muscles; spasms may be painful. They may be triggered by sudden submersion in cold water, overexertion, or improper seating. Spasms cannot be controlled once they start and one must wait until the movement stops.

## MUSCULAR DYSTROPHY

A progressive disease resulting in weakening of the muscles with decreased muscle tone. Watch for fatigue.

## PARAPLEGIA

Some degree of paralysis and/or loss of sensation in both legs and possibly lower parts of the body; may have muscle spasms in the legs. Paraplegia usually results from injury or disease affecting the spinal cord from the T-1 level or below. (Appendix 2)

## PHLEBITIS

Swelling in a vein.

## PROSTHESIS

Artificial limb or artificial substitute for a missing body part.

## PSYCHOTROPIC DRUGS

Drugs that affect the mental functions or behavior.

## QUADRIPLEGIA

Some degree of impairment of muscles and/or sensation with paralysis in all four limbs. Trunk stability may be affected. May have some use of arms but reduced hand function. May have muscle spasms.

## SENSATION

Ability to feel sensory stimuli such as touch, pain, heat or cold. Sensory loss may be total or partial.

## SPASTICITY

Hyperactive muscles which move involuntarily. See Muscle Spasms.

## SPINA BIFIDA

Birth defect of spine and spinal cord; may result in weakness and loss of sensation or complete paralysis of legs below the level of the defect on the spine.

## SPINAL CORD INJURY OR DISEASE

A spinal cord injury is referred to by its level, e.g. a C-6 quadriplegic has her injury at the sixth cervical vertebra.(Appendix 2)

## STUMP

The part of the limb remaining after amputation.

## TRANSFER

Movement from one surface to another; usually refers to moving to/from wheelchair, e.g. moving from wheelchair to the boat.

## TREMOR

An involuntary trembling movement; this is often seen in people with Multiple Sclerosis, and Parkinson's disease.

## TRUNK STABILITY/BALANCE IN SITTING

Trunk muscles which allow a person to stand or sit unsupported are weakened or absent in some conditions. Therefore, the person is unable to balance herself without support.

## UPPER EXTREMITIES

Refers to arms.

## VISUAL IMPAIRMENT

Loss of some ability to see, either partial or complete. Many people with visual impairment have some sight. Some people see lines, shapes or colors; others can detect only light and shadow.

# SPINAL COLUMN

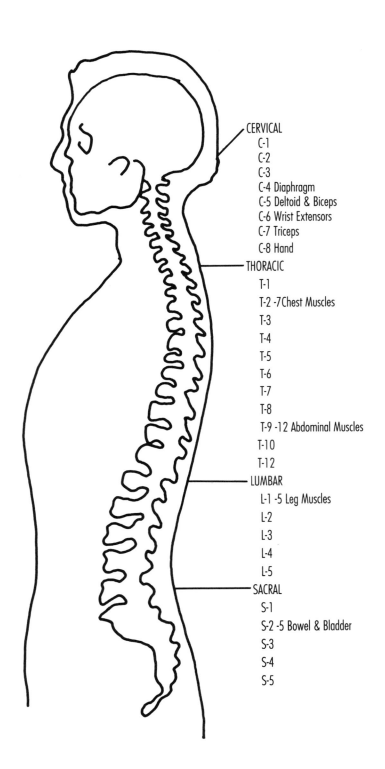

CERVICAL
C-1
C-2
C-3
C-4 Diaphragm
C-5 Deltoid & Biceps
C-6 Wrist Extensors
C-7 Triceps
C-8 Hand
THORACIC
T-1
T-2 -7 Chest Muscles
T-3
T-4
T-5
T-6
T-7
T-8
T-9 -12 Abdominal Muscles
T-10
T-12
LUMBAR
L-1 -5 Leg Muscles
L-2
L-3
L-4
L-5
SACRAL
S-1
S-2 -5 Bowel & Bladder
S-3
S-4
S-5

A person with a spinal cord injury may be a paraplegic or a quadriplegic. When spinal cord injury occurs, the level is designated, for example, a *C-4 quadriplegia*. Paraplegia results from injury at the T-1 (thoracic) level or below, and quadriplegia results from injury at the C-8 (cervical) level or above.

Neurological damage may be <u>COMPLETE</u> with no sensation or movement, or <u>INCOMPLETE</u> with varying degrees of sensation or motion.

If the lesion is <u>COMPLETE</u>, the following applies:
- C-6 to C-8 - impairment of hand and lower arm use. Some people may be able to grasp paddle, but not have full hand motion.
- T-6 - muscles below the nipple-line are effected.
- T-8 and above - eliminates most balance while sitting.
- T-9 to T-12 - eliminates abdominal muscles for rotating trunk and forward flexion of trunk. Loss of some abdominal muscles also affects balance.
- Lumbar and sacral lesions affect leg muscles; torso and balance remain intact.

If the lesion is <u>INCOMPLETE</u>, these effects will vary with the individual.

# MEDICAL INFORMATION SHEET

Canoeing/kayaking is a strenuous activity. If you have questions regarding your health and participation in canoeing/kayaking, please discuss it with your physician. We ask you for the following information to be aware of potential problems and to help you to enjoy safely canoeing/kayaking. Please use the back if needed.

Name_____Telephone_____

Address_____

_____

Height_____Weight_____ Date of Birth_____

**Yes**    **No**    **Have you ever had?** (*Please check the appropriate column.*)

____ ____ Allergies If yes, to what? _____

____ ____ Diabetes

____ ____ Heart Disease

____ ____ Epilepsy

____ ____ Asthma

____ ____ High Blood Pressure

____ ____ Back Problems

____ ____ Dislocations If yes, which joint(s)_____

____ ____ Seizures?  If yes, what tends to trigger them?_____

____ ____ Do you get cold easily?

____ ____ Are you affected greatly by the heat?

____ ____ Are you pregnant?

____ ____ Are you taking medication?

            What type?_____

            What side effects, such as fatigue or sensitivity to the sun, do they have?_____

____ ____ Are you allergic to any medication?

____ ____ Do you have muscle spasms? If yes, what tends to trigger them?

            _____

            If yes, what type?_____

____ ____ Are you allergic to insect bites and stings?

            If yes, what medication do you carry? _____

____ ____ Are there any limitations to your activities?

            If yes, what are they? _____

Page 2
Describe your swimming ability.

Describe your canoeing/kayaking experience.

How would you describe your general health?

Insurance Company _____Group Number _____

Insured person's name _____

In case of emergency, notify:
Name:_____Phone_____
Name:_____Phone_____
Name:_____Phone_____

Additional comments:

This form is based on the health form used by the Nantahala Outdoor Center.

# OPPORTUNITIES FOR PADDLING INSTRUCTION AND TRIPS

**American Canoe Association**
P.O. Box 1190
Newington, VA 22122-1190
(703) 550-7495

Certified instructors throughout the country.

**Challenge Alaska**
P.O. Box 110065
Anchorage, AL 99511
(907) 563-2658

Sea kayaking trips.

**Cooperative Wilderness Handicapped Outdoor Group (C.W. Hog)**
Idaho State University Student Union
Box 8118
Pocatello, ID 83209
(208) 236-3912

University based adventure programming. A broad program which encourages adventure to each individual's limit.

**Environmental Traveling Companions (ETC)**
Fort Mason Center
Landmark Building C
San Francisco, CA 94123
(415) 474-7662

Able/disabled day and overnight trips in the San Francisco area only.

**Maui Sea Kayaking**
P.O. Box 106
Puunene, HI 96784
(808) 572-6299 Contact Ron Bass.

Sea kayaking and canoeing instruction and able/disabled trips.

**Nantahala Outdoor Center**
US 19W, Box 41
Bryson City, NC 28713
(704) 488-2175

Instruction for able and disabled in whitewater kayaking, including Eskimo roll.

**Pacific Water Sports**
c/o Tim Davis
16205 Pacific Hwy South
Seattle, WA 98188
(206) 246-9385

Kayaking instruction available.
Contact Tim for information on the Summer Splash Program. Water sports for people with disabilities.

**Regatta Challenge**
Information and Registration - Contact:
American Paralysis Association
2149 Seville Ave.
Balboa, CA 92661

Kayak Race - able and disabled
Competition at all levels of experience in the fall yearly
in Newport Beach, CA

**Shared Adventures, Inc.**
c/o Kent Winchester
76 Eastland Avenue
Rochester, NY 14618
(716) 442-8104

Able/disabled canoe and kayak trips in the Adirondacks and Canada.

**SOAR (Shared Outdoor Adventure Recreation)**
P.O. Box 14583
Portland, OR 97214
(503) 238-1613.

Sea kayaking instruction and tours on Oregon rivers in August and September.

**S'PLORE** (Special Populations Learning Outdoor Recreation and Education)
699 East South Temple, Suite 120
Salt Lake City, UT 84102
(801) 363-7130.

Flatwater canoeing and whitewater rafting.

**Vinland National Center**
3675 Ihduhapi Road
P.O. Box 308
Loretto, MN 55357
(612) 479-3555

Sports and recreation information for persons with disabilities.

**Wilderness Inquiry**
1313 Fifth Street, SE
Suite 327 A
Minneapolis, MN 55414
(612) 379-3858

Canoe and sea kayaking trips - able/disabled - nationally and internationally.

# RESOURCES

Arthur, Michael and Stacy Ackroyd-Stolarz. <u>A Resource Manual on Canoeing for Disabled People</u>. Canadian Recreational Canoeing Association; P.O. Box 500, Hyde Park, Ontario, Canada NOM1Z0, (519) 473-2109.

Bechdel, Les and Slim Ray. <u>River Rescue</u>. Boston, MA: Appalachian Mountain Club, 1985.

Dowd, John. <u>Sea Kayaking, A Manual for Long-Distance Touring</u>. Vancouver, British Columbia: Douglas and McIntyre, Ltd.,1988.

Evans, Eric and Jay. <u>The Kayaking Book</u>. Lexington, MA: The Stephen Greene Press, 1988.

Galland, John. <u>Introduction to Kayaking for Persons with Disabilities</u>. Vinland National Center, 3675 Ihduhapi Road, P.O. Box 308, Loretto, MN 55357.

Gullion, Laurie. <u>Canoeing and Kayaking, Instruction Manual</u>. American Canoe Association, Inc., P.O. Box 1190, Newington, VA 22122, 1987.

Hutchinson, Derek. <u>Eskimo Rolling</u>. Camden, ME: International Marine Publishing Company, 1988.

Hutchinson, Derek. <u>Sea Canoeing</u>. London: A and C Black, 1985.

Price, Bruce, ed. <u>Fundamentals of Coastal Kayaking Manual for Instructors</u>, American Canoe Association, Inc., P.O. Box 1190, Newington, VA 22122-1190, 1989.

Smedley, Geoff. <u>A Guide to Canoeing With Disabled Persons</u>. British Canoe Union, Mapperley Hall, Lucknow Avenue, Nottingham, England, NG3 5FA.

Walbridge, Charles. <u>Boatbuilder's Manual</u>. Birmingham, Alabama: Menasha Ridge Press, 1987.

Washburne, Randel. <u>The Coastal Kayaker, Kayak Camping on the Alaska and B.C. Coast</u>. Seattle, WA: Pacific Search Press, 1983.

<u>River Safety Report 1986-1988</u>, Charles C. Walbridge, ed., American Canoe Association, Newington, VA, 1989.

<u>Canoeing and Kayaking</u>, The American National Red Cross, USA, 1981.

**Magazines:**

American Canoeist
American Canoe Association, Inc.
P.O. Box 1190
Newington, VA 22122

American Whitewater
AWA Journal
146 N. Brockway
Palatine, IL 60067

Canoe
P.O. Box 10748
Des Moines, IA 50349-0748

Canoesport Journal
American Canoesport Inc.
P.O. Box 991
Odessa, FL 33556
(813) 938-6191

River Runner
P.O. Box 697
Fallbrook, CA 92028

Sea Kayaker
1670 Duranleau Street,
Vancouver, B.C. V6H 3S4

Sports 'N Spokes
5201 North 19th Avenue,
Suite 111,
Phoenix, AZ 85015

# SOURCES FOR ADAPTATIONS

American Canoe Association
Disabled Paddlers' Committee
P.O. Box 1190
Newington, VA 22122-1190
(703) 550-7495

American Foundation for the Blind
15 West 16th Street
New York, NY 10011
(201) 862-8838.

Cleo, Inc.
3957 Mayfield Road
Cleveland, OH 44121
(800) 321-0595

The Coleman Company
P.O. Box 11706
Wichita, KS 67201
(800) 835-3278

Crazy Creek Products
P.O. Box 896
Red Lodge, MT 59068

Essex Industries
Pelfisher Road
Mineville, NY 12956

Hardbody Fitness Systems, Inc.
"Firm Fist Grip"
22600 B-Lambert, Suite 807
El Toro, CA 92630
(714) 768-8070

L.L. Bean
Freeport, ME 04033

Mad River Canoe
Box 610
Waitsfield, VT 05673
(802) 496-3127

Rion Acoustic Instruments, Inc.
912 West 223rd St.
Torrance, CA 90502

TAP Plastics
3011 Alvarado Street
San Leandro, CA

TRS, Inc.
1280 28th Street,
Suite 3
Boulder, CO 80303-1797

Wildwater Designs
230 Penllyn Pike
Penllyn, PA 19422
(215) 646-5034

Yakima
P.O. Box 4899
Arcata, CA 95521
(707) 826-8000

# BIBLIOGRAPHY

Arthur, Michael and Stacy Ackroyd-Stolarz. <u>A Resource Manual on Canoeing For Disabled People</u>. Canadian Recreational Canoeing Association, P.O. Box 500, Hyde Park, Ontario, Canada, NOM1Z0.

Galland, John. <u>Introduction to Kayaking for Persons with Disabilities</u>. Vinland National Center, 3675 Ihduhapi Road, P.O. Box 308, Loretto, MN 55357.

Gullion, Laurie. <u>Canoeing and Kayaking, Instruction Manual</u>. American Canoe Association, Inc., P.O. Box 1190, Newington, VA 22122, 1987.

Hutchinson, Derek. <u>Eskimo Rolling</u>. Camden, ME: International Marine Publishing Company, 1988.

Smedley, Geoff. <u>A Guide to Canoeing With Disabled Persons</u>. British Canoe Union, Mapperley Hall, Lucknow Avenue, Nottingham, England, NG3 5FA.

Walbridge, Charles. <u>Boatbuilder's Manual</u>. Birmingham, AL: Menasha Ridge Press, 1987.

<u>Canoeing and Kayaking</u>. The American Red Cross. USA, 1981.

<u>International Directory of Recreation Oriented Assistive Devices</u>. Life Boat Press, Box 11782, Marina Del Rey, CA 90295.

<u>Watersports for the Disabled</u>. British Sports Association for the Disabled. Water Sports Division, East Ardsley, England: E. P. Publishing, Ltd., 1983.

# INDEX